MW01680914

On The Same Page

800+ Questions for LGBTQ+ Couples

By Sammi & Heydee

Dedicated to our 20s

This book is a work of nonfiction. The content is intended for informational and conversational purposes only and is not a substitute for professional therapy, counseling, or medical advice.

Published by Sammi and Heydee
Printed in the United States by Amazon KDP

First edition
ISBN: 979-8-218-88021-7

TABLE OF CONTENTS

HOW TO USE THIS BOOK

Communication is often the difference between feeling deeply connected and feeling misunderstood. Too many couples go years without asking the questions that matter: questions that could have clarified expectations, prevented conflict, or even saved a relationship. This book is here to help make sure those conversations happen. ***Here's how we recommend using it:***

Go at Your Own Pace

There is no right way to read this book. Start wherever feels most relevant to you. Skip around, revisit sections, or take it page by page. Some questions may be lighthearted; others might bring up feelings. Give each other space to reflect and respond without rushing the process.

Make It a Conversation, Not an Interview

This book is meant to help you have meaningful conversations, not to control how you talk, what you say, or what your relationship should look like. Take turns asking and answering, and focus on understanding, not agreement. Listen fully, respond honestly, and let the conversations evolve naturally.

Let It Be a Guide, Not a Rulebook

Not every question will apply to your relationship, and that's okay! Use what resonates, modify what you need to make it your own, and skip anything that doesn't serve you.

INTRODUCTION

Nine years with someone will teach you a lot: the biggest lesson? **Love alone is not enough.**

Heydee and I have spent our entire 20s together. And if there's one thing about your 20s, it's that life stops going the way you pictured it. You question everything: your choices, your priorities, the person you thought you'd become. Your identity develops. Your perspective evolves. And your sense of self becomes either crystal clear or completely unrecognizable.

And none of it happens in isolation.

•••

Change spills into relationships.

It seeps into the cracks and pushes things apart, slowly shifting the ground beneath you. For most people the shift is subtle.

It settles into the rhythm of everyday life: where affection starts to feel platonic, conversations become predictable, and conflict gets postponed until it fades into resentment. Little by little the space between you widens. And not because of one big thing, but a thousand small ones.

You move in different directions. And then one day you look up and realize you're standing in two different places.

The reality is, growth doesn't care about your timeline. Change is inevitable. The question is not if it ***will*** happen. It's **when.**

•••

In the queer community, relationships move fast. There's even a joke about it: ***U-hauling.*** One moment, you're on your first date; next, you're picking out furniture and planning a future.

The honeymoon phase is great. Everything feels effortless. Then your lives start to merge. That's when the real stuff surfaces: like how you handle stress and how you see the world. The questions you never thought to ask start to matter. And the conversations you didn't know you needed become the ones you can't avoid.

For us, that moment came during the pandemic. It forced us into a corner. There was no buffer between us anymore. No personal space.

Lockdown stripped everything away: the routines, the excuses. And all that was left was us. Just two people trying not to lose it in a world that had already gone off the rails.

We argued more than ever.

Some days it felt like that's all we did. *But breaking up during a pandemic?* That was a whole different kind of impossible. *Where would we go? Who would we be without each other in a world that had come to a halt?* It was like being thrown into couples therapy without a therapist. The small stuff became big, and the big stuff felt impossible.

Once our routines disappeared, we were forced to confront our relationship problems: how we avoided, how we fought. Being together 24/7 magnified our issues. And we had to ask ourselves if we were still in it, or just afraid to let go.

It was the biggest challenge of our relationship, but eventually we adapted. We gave each other room to change, and through small adjustments and big conversations, we started to rebuild what we had nearly lost.

•••

During those rocky phases, we searched for guidance.

We wanted something to help us make sense of what we were going through. Something relatable. But most of what we found was created for heterosexual couples, with assumptions that didn't reflect our reality.

The books, the articles, and the late-night Google searches all spoke to dynamics we did not see in ourselves.

The roles and expectations were different. And while we leaned on friends when we could, some topics felt too intimate or too complicated to share. We wanted something that felt like us. Something that mirrored our experiences.

That's why we wrote this book.

Whether you're just starting out, years in, or somewhere in between, ***we hope this book helps you have the conversations that matter most.***

GOALS & DREAMS

INTRODUCTION

Wanting something and being willing to do what it takes to get it are not the same thing. It's easy to want shit. Everyone wants more money. More time. Wanting *isn't* special.

It's execution that separates you. Dreams require action. They require structure, sacrifice, and an actual plan. They cost you sleep. Stability. Sometimes even relationships. Whatever it is, there will always be a price. Everything you want will cost you something. But the most expensive thing you'll ever pay for is wasted potential.

•••

One of the hardest things you will ever face in life is the gap between knowing what you want and actually doing what it takes to get there. It's one of the most frustrating parts of being human.

Some people face it late in life. The sadness that comes with looking back at everything they didn't do. Some experience it halfway through a crisis, when it's too late to act. And some are strong enough to confront it early.

For as long as I can remember, I've struggled with the distance between what I know and what I do. My constant choice to do what feels good now instead of what I know will move me forward.

To be honest, substance use has played a bigger role in this than I like to admit.

I've hit goals. I've accomplished things. But most of them came in short, inspired bursts, rarely from long-term discipline. I used to think I could outsmart consistency, that success would come if I just wanted it badly enough. And sometimes, it did. But I was high through most of it.

That's the part that stings.

•••

A lot of people have a pretty narrow view of substance use. They picture someone non-functional, life completely in shambles. Someone who's hit rock bottom. But spend enough time around substances and you realize the connection is a lot more complex. It's subtle.

Drugs don't destroy your life overnight.

They maneuver their way into everything. You can function. You can get shit done. You can show up for your friends. But they're in the background of every celebration and every self-destructive spiral. They're the angel talking you through the hard times and the devil keeping you stuck in them.

And because they're tied to so many of your experiences, letting them go feels like losing a piece of yourself.

•••

Here's what I've learned: your brain prioritizes relief over your goals. And the fastest path to relief is almost never the path forward.

Substances taught me this lesson better than anything else. Every battle you fight in life comes back to the same one: *you against yourself.* It comes down to discipline and willpower. The two most valuable traits a person can have. And there is no clearer example of this fight within yourself than being someone who knows what's right while reaching for something you know is wrong.

•••

I'm still somewhere in between knowing and doing.

Some days I choose progress. But there are also days I spend several hours on social media, avoiding what matters and convincing myself I'll reset tomorrow. That I need my vices for now, because of how heavy life feels. That I'll quit when life calms down. Deep down though, I know I don't need them. I know I'm capable of more.

I lost my income, my confidence, and my pride. I could no longer help my parents out financially. There were no more date nights. No more little luxuries.

The worst part was having to look my younger siblings in the eye and explain why I couldn't get them anything for their birthdays. That shit really pulled at my heartstrings.

Yet as devastating as it was, the experience became a catalyst for some of the most important lessons of my life. I have my failures to thank for the version of myself I am today which is a better version of who I used to be.

•••

Failure is often mistaken for the opposite of progress, when in fact it's an essential input. Our brains learn best through error correction. Progress comes from analyzing what went wrong, not from avoiding it altogether.

The problem isn't failure itself. It's our refusal to sit with it and extract the lessons.

When you start viewing failure as feedback rather than a verdict, you develop real resilience. It stops feeling personal and starts becoming practical. You actually learn from your failures, and in doing so they become useful. They turn into perspective, helping you make better choices and understand yourself more.

I've failed a lot. But I embrace it now. The way I see it, every failure puts me closer to a win. And when I fall short, I don't ignore my mistakes. I pull them apart to see what went wrong. The why, the when, the how. My failures have become a part of my process, not an interruption to it.

As my relationship with failure has evolved, so has my definition of success. My goals have gone from external to internal, with the understanding that the goals I accomplish internally will affect my outcomes externally.

I used to want to be someone impressive. Now I want to be someone grounded.

•••

I've been honest with Heydee about my goals. All of them.

Even the ones I'm embarrassed about. Even the ones I've failed at more times than I can count, like quitting something I've already quit a dozen times before.

If you're pursuing anything worth having, you're going to fall short. Nobody reaches their goals in a straight line. You will repeat mistakes. And admitting them to the person you love is hard. But it's necessary. Because there's no rule for how many times it should take to get something right. No set number of relapses or resets before you stop being worthy of trying again.

The difference between a goal and an accomplishment lies in your ability to keep showing up, even when you feel ashamed.

•••

There are few things in a relationship as intimate as talking about your goals and dreams. The real ones. The ones that feel personal and hard to put into words. Sharing them is like offering a glimpse of the person you hope to grow into, the version of yourself you're reaching toward.

And if you don't know what your partner is reaching toward, a part of them will remain out of reach.

•••

Although our paths to this point have been different, Heydee and I have learned to move forward side by side.

I know her struggles, her dreams, and the life she's building. She knows my fears, my motivations, and the goals that matter most to me… even the ones I've failed at more than once. She knows when I'm trying again, and she meets my effort with compassion.

We've stopped waiting for life to be smooth to *"feel successful"*. There will always be changes and challenges. That's not failure. **That's being alive.**

Success, for us, is defined by resilience.

It's about being able to hold each other steady when the ground moves and trusting that we'll find our footing again. And every time, we get a little better at it.

•••

The truth is, you've got what it takes.

The difference between you and someone who's already living their dream is that they took action. They made the decision to start, to try, and to keep showing up. Your dreams are worth pursuing, whatever they may be. You don't need permission or a perfect plan.

You just need courage: *the courage to keep choosing the life you want, even if you're still becoming the person who can live it.*

Defining Goals

Overcoming Challenges

Building Our Future

DEFINING GOALS

01.
What are three goals you're currently working toward, and what motivates you most when working toward a goal?

02.
Do you have a clear timeline for your goals?

3.
hich of these goals do you see as personal, and which
ou see as shared goals for us as a couple?

u measure success in your life?

wed you around for a week, would they
ious about your goals?

06.

What's a long-term goal that you're willing to sacrifice short-term comfort or happiness for, and why?

07.

Are there any goals you've put off or given up on in the past that you'd like to revisit?

08.

What milestones or achievements do you hope we'll celebrate together in the next few years?

09.

If your younger self could see your life now, would they be proud, disappointed, or confused?

10.

With unlimited resources and no obstacles, what passion or dream would you pursue today?

OVERCOMING CHALLENGES

11.
How would you feel if your dream required us to take a risk that could drastically alter our lives or financial situation?

12.
What goal of yours do you think I don't take seriously?

13.
If one of us feels the other isn't pulling their weight toward achieving a shared goal, how should we address it?

14.
Do you feel like I support you when you're working toward your goals?

15.
How often would you like me to check in with you about your goals—daily, weekly, or just when it comes up?

16.
If we reach a point where one of our goals requires the other to sacrifice something significant, how do we decide which sacrifices are worth making?

17.
Can we identify any recurring influences, such as social circles, family expectations, or personal habits, that tend to derail us from our goals, either individually or as a couple?

18.
What's the biggest obstacle you've faced when working toward something important?

19.
Have you ever felt like you couldn't celebrate a win because I was struggling—or vice versa ?

20.
What's a goal you've outgrown but still feel pressure to achieve—either from yourself, me, or others?

BUILDING OUR FUTURE

21.
Do you feel like we are taking practical steps to achieve our goals?

22.
What does "retirement" look like to you? *(e.g., relaxing, traveling, or working part-time?)*

23.
What's a realistic balance between time spent working toward our goals and time just relaxing together?

24.
What habit do you think separates people who succeed from those who don't?

25.
Do you think people are more motivated by where they want to go, or by what they're trying to escape?

26.
What do you imagine our life looking like 10 years from now?

27.
What's one thing we'd regret not doing together in the next 10 years, and how can we make it happen?

28.
What kind of lifestyle do we want to have in the future—do we picture ourselves traveling, settling down, or something else?

29.
Do you measure success by what you have, what you've accomplished, or who you've become?

30.
When you imagine growing old with me, what are the things you hope we never stop doing?

MORALS & BELIEFS

INTRODUCTION

As a kid, I often found myself puzzled by my mom.

I never understood why we had to sit through Michael Moore documentaries in theaters when I'd rather be playing outside. I didn't understand why she insisted on marching at protests, or why she refused to take off that ***"Free Palestine"*** bumper sticker, even when it made us a target.

One summer, a man followed our car for miles. At first, I thought it was a coincidence. But when we pulled into a gas station, he pulled in too. He stormed up to us and started yelling: ranting about our bumper sticker and about how people like us didn't exist.

I was so confused. ***Like, what do you mean we don't exist? I'm literally standing in front of you.***

Later, I found out he didn't believe Palestine was a real place, and therefore that Palestinians had no ***"legitimacy."*** I wondered why she didn't scrape the sticker off that day. But she didn't. She stood there calmly and told me to get back in the car. When it was over, we drove off like it was familiar. Like it belonged to a long history of moments she knew all too well.

As I got older, these moments became familiar to me too.

Growing up with a Palestinian mom and a Jewish dad comes with its own set of questions and obligations.

Questions like: *Whose side are you on?* As if my Jewish heritage obligates me to side with the oppressor. Or as if my Palestinian heritage wouldn't come with an awareness and understanding of Israeli propaganda, or as if years of witnessing suffering and hearing stories from my family wouldn't strengthen my stance altogether.

Sometimes I'd avoid telling people I was Palestinian. I didn't like the attention or the change in behavior when someone found out. It made people uncomfortable—which, in turn, made me uncomfortable.

But over time, I developed a stronger sense of duty. A duty to speak up, to represent Palestinians with pride, and to teach others about our land and our history.

And a duty to the Jewish community to draw a clear distinction and understanding that the acts of Israel and of zionists do not reflect the beliefs and values of the Jewish people.

Confusing the two only increases division at a time when unity and understanding are desperately needed.

I come from a lineage of conviction. I grew up watching people in my family sacrifice a lot for what they believed in. I learned pretty young what it means to stand firm in your values. I was raised to understand that our beliefs are only as strong as our willingness to carry them into uncomfortable places.

Eventually, these lessons turned into my instincts that shaped both my relationships and my sense of self. And my moral code became part of the lens I see people through.

I have a few non-negotiables: I could never date someone who is a zionist, racist, transphobic, supports ICE, isn't pro-choice, or aligns with Republican views. Beyond politics and principle, I draw the line at cruelty: whether that looks like mocking someone who's struggling or treating others as if they only exist to serve you. To me, these things are the clearest sign of a person's character.

Who you support and how you treat people when you have nothing to gain says everything about who you are.

Heydee and I are different in the ways that keep life interesting. But despite all the surface-level differences, we've always shared the same instincts. She supports the rights and freedoms of all individuals. She is the first to stand up to a bully, and she won't hesitate to attend a protest. She pays attention. She cares in the same way I do.

This is why we work.

The things that matter to you say everything about who you are. The way you treat your loved ones. The way you treat strangers. Whether you participate. What movements you stand with. What change you believe in. These are ethical truths. They reflect the way you see yourself. What we believe shapes what we choose. And what we choose, again and again, becomes who we are.

•••

Life will test you. It will stretch your patience and challenge your principles. It will expose every gap between your intentions and your actions. And in those moments, love by itself won't sustain you. What will is knowing you're with someone who believes in the same core truths: whose perspective may differ from yours but is anchored in similar principles.

A relationship can survive different tastes in television, different hobbies, different routines. *But core values?* These are the bones. The blueprint. The understanding that lets you move through life together without having to explain the things that should already make sense.

Love begins with emotion, but it's sustained by intention. You choose your values. You choose your priorities. And when you share those choices with someone else, they influence not only your relationship, but the person you're becoming within it.

Moral & Ethical Values

Trust & Attraction

Religion & Beliefs

Social Justice

Messy Dilemmas

MORAL & ETHICAL VALUES

31.
What is one value that you hold above all others, and why is it important to you? *(e.g., honesty, loyalty, independence, kindness, growth, family.)*

32.
Do you feel it's your responsibility to constantly work on improving yourself, or are you satisfied with who you are right now?

33.
Do you think honesty should always outweigh kindness?

34.
Would you tell the truth to someone even if it meant hurting their feelings?

35.
Is withholding information the same as lying?

36.
Do you believe everyone deserves a second chance—or are there some actions you think are unforgivable?

37.
Is filming a stranger in public unethical if they're doing something harmful, embarrassing, or *going viral-worthy*?

38.
Would you stay friends with someone if their morals didn't align with yours? What's the deal-breaker for you?

39.
Would you cover for someone you love, even if they committed a serious crime?

40.
If you had to choose between saving someone you've never met or your lifelong pet, which would you pick?

TRUST & ATTRACTION

41.
How do you define privacy in a relationship, and what boundaries are important for you to feel respected?

42.
Would you be open to sharing your location with me, and how would you feel if one of us wasn't comfortable with it?

43.
Have you ever lost attraction because you lost trust? Or lost trust because you lost attraction?

44.
What do you consider a "dealbreaker" in a relationship, and have your dealbreakers changed over time?

45.
When you notice a red flag in your relationship, do you bring it up right away or wait until you're sure it's a problem?

46.
Who do you trust the most and the least in your life right now? And why?

47.
Do you trust people until they give you a reason not to, or do they have to earn it first?

48.
Would knowing the exact number of people I've slept with change how you see me, and why?

49.
What personal boundary do you hold when it comes to interacting with people you might feel attracted to?

50.
What's the difference between admiring someone and finding them attractive?

51.
Can our romantic relationship thrive without sexual attraction?

52.
Do you believe physical effort (like hygiene or dressing up) should be equal in a relationship?

53.
What do you think I struggle to see in myself that you find incredibly attractive? And what type of compliments from me would make you feel more attractive?

54.
If you were attracted to someone at work, or if a coworker hit on you, would you feel obligated to tell me?

RELIGION & BELIEFS

55.
Do you believe in God or a higher power, and how does your faith or spirituality influence your daily life?

56.
Could you date someone with a different religious viewpoint, and how important is it for you to share similar beliefs with your partner?

57.
Are there any non-negotiables in your beliefs that a partner must respect, even if they don't agree?

58.
What role, if any, should religion or spirituality play in our relationship?

59.
How do you navigate religious holidays, and are you open to celebrating holidays from other religions?

60.
How has your faith or belief system changed over time? And Would you ever consider changing or adapting your beliefs for a partner?

61.
How would you feel if I started exploring a new religion or spiritual path, and it eventually came with commitments—like going to church, changing routines, or following certain practices?

62.
Do you think religion has done more harm or more good in the world?

63.
Is it ever okay to challenge or question someone else's beliefs? If so, when and how?

64.
Is it ethical to try to convert someone to your belief system? Why or why not?

SOCIAL JUSTICE

66.
Is it possible to be neutral on issues of justice, or is silence always taking a side?

67.
Would you risk your comfort to stand up for someone else's rights?

68.
Is it ethical to vote for your own benefit if it harms others?

69.
When does calling someone out become public shaming instead of accountability?

70.
If one of us has more privilege, resources, or social power than the other, how do we make sure that power isn't used in ways that hurt the other? *(like in arguments, breakups, or public situations?)*

71.
If your partner's career requires choices that clash with your ethics, do you expect them to prioritize your values over their job?

72.
Is it wrong to stay silent when you hear friends or family say something harmful, like racist, sexist, or homophobic comments?

73.
What social issues matter most to you, and do you engage in politics or activism?

74.
What responsibilities do we have to our community and society?

75.
When your partner's family or friends hold values or beliefs you fundamentally disagree with, how much effort should you make to get along with them—and at what point does that effort cross into compromising your own morals?

MESSY DILEMMAS

76.
Do we have the kind of relationship where we can point out when someone is hot without the other getting offended?

77.
Would you tell your partner if their friend hit on you?

78.
Is it wrong to flirt with someone for access, free drinks, or other perks if you're in a relationship?

79.
Have you ever hooked up with someone who was in a relationship or married?

80.
Would you feel comfortable dating someone who creates adult content?

81.
Is it wrong to date someone who looks exactly like your ex?

82.
What are your boundaries around dating people your friends have dated?

83.
How would you feel if a friend dated someone you once dated or hooked up with?

84.
Would you stay friends with someone who openly disliked your partner?

85.
If you hit a parked car and no one saw, would you leave a note?

CONFLICT & ARGUMENTS

INTRODUCTION

From screaming matches across the street to throwing hands in our apartment, Samantha and I have had our fair share of fights. I won't pretend otherwise. We've really fought. Moments I'd be embarrassed to talk about.

Real shit we both cringe over whenever it comes up.

My parents got married at 24, and I was born not long after. Our families never really got along, but once I was born they were forced to try and hold it together... for a while, at least. Some of my earliest memories are of them fighting, mostly my dad being a dick. When they divorced, I became the thing they argued over, trapped in the crossfire of a custody battle.

In Iran, fathers automatically get custody unless the mother can offer something more valuable. My mom gave up her house for me. It was a home passed down from her father. That was the trade: me for a house.

After they divorced, my mom met a man who later became my stepdad. He moved us to America, and for a while, life felt good. He was kind, he loved my mom, and he loved me like his own daughter. He taught me English. Every day, he would read me Harry Potter and have me write the same word over and over again until it felt natural in my hand.

He worked full-time and even after a long day, he still managed to make time for little adventures. My favorite memory of him is when he took us to the Natural History Museum. He was so excited, pointing things out and trying to explain them to me. I learned so much that day. Afterward, he took us to Subway for sandwiches, and we ate them on a rock in Central Park and people-watched. That day meant everything to me. He was the father figure I needed at the time. Then, out of nowhere, he got cancer and passed away. And just like that, it was me and my mom.

My adolescence was rough.

Being Middle Eastern in America was hard enough on its own, but it was especially hard in the years after 9/11. I got bullied a lot. And the media didn't help. Everywhere I looked, people who looked like me were either the villain or the punchline.

I was too young to fully understand it, but I could sense it. The suspicion. The side-eyes. The way people flinched at my name or paused when they heard my mom's accent.

School was the worst. I had long hair and a unibrow. Even my arms were hairy. I looked different from the other kids in class, and they made sure I knew it. They called me names like *"Hairy Hyena"* and *"Hideous."* They even called me a *"terrorist."*

It was brutal.

I hardly knew enough English to ask where the bathroom was, let alone defend myself. Without the words or the confidence to let it slide, fighting became my only option. And conflict became my first language.

•••

Samantha and I grew up in completely different worlds, and we both came into this relationship carrying baggage from our past.

While my childhood taught me to meet conflict head-on, she grew up in a household where yelling was normal and arguments always escalated. She learned early to shut down and internalize her feelings, avoiding difficult conversations until avoidance was no longer an option. When we met, those patterns clashed. I escalated quickly because I felt overlooked, and Samantha withdrew because confrontation felt unsafe.

But eventually, we realized something important: you can't fix what you refuse to acknowledge. Understanding that was the real work. For me, it meant learning to pause, to breathe, and to actually listen. For Samantha, it meant expressing herself without sounding condescending and stepping away when she needed to cool off.

How you learned to argue follows you into every conflict.

It becomes your default. It decides whether you push to make your point or step back to protect yourself. It influences your tone, your body language, and how you handle love in moments of stress.

But what was normal then doesn't have to be normal now. Your reactions, your defenses, your instinct to fight or avoid—none of them appeared from nowhere. They were learned, which means they can be unlearned and replaced with something healthier.

This process starts with awareness: noticing your triggers and deciding what outcome you want *before* you speak.

Use language that invites honest dialogue. Take pauses that create space for resolution. Change happens when you refuse to repeat what no longer serves you. And sometimes a single choice toward something better can be the turning point your life has been waiting for.

Improving Communication

Rules & Boundaries

Infidelity

Aftermath & Rebuilding

IMPROVING COMMUNICATION

85.
What kinds of situations and conversations tend to trigger conflict between us?

86.
When we argue, what are the common patterns we fall into? (shutting down, raising voices, sarcasm)

87.
Do you think one of us tends to dominate arguments, leaving the other feeling unheard or dismissed?

88.
Would you say one of us is better at moving on without needing closure?

89.
What is my role in escalating or de-escalating conflict?

90.
What do you think is the difference between healthy expressions of anger and harmful behaviors like verbal abuse?

91.
Do you feel more confident resolving conflict with me than with others? Why or why not?

92.
Do you believe we can improve how we argue? If so, what changes would help us communicate better during disagreements?

93.
What feels worse to you: being interrupted, being misunderstood, or being ignored?

94.
Do you believe tone matters more than words, or do words matter more than tone during conflict?

RULES & BOUNDARIES

95.
Is it okay to seek advice from friends during a conflict? What boundaries should we have to help protect our privacy and each other's dignity?

96.
How would you feel if I called your parents after an argument to get their perspective on what happened?

97.
How do you feel about addressing conflict in front of others—are you okay with it or do you prefer privacy?

98.
Are there triggers we should be more mindful of, or topics and behaviors that should be off-limits during conflict?

99.
Do you think it's fair to bring up old conflicts during current arguments to justify our feelings?

100.
Should we have a rule about avoiding arguments at certain times, like before work, before bed, or before important events?

101.
Should we set a rule around how often we bring up issues—like not unloading multiple complaints back to back?

102.
What kinds of comments feel impossible for you to "unhear," even after an apology?

103.
How much conflict feels normal or healthy to you in a relationship, and how much would start to feel like a red flag?

104.
What signs tell us that an argument has stopped being productive or safe—and what behaviors should signal it's time to take a break?

105.
Should we set a rule about not making major relationship decisions (like breaking up) in the heat of an argument?

106.
What's the most respectful and effective way for us to call each other out when things start getting petty, passive-aggressive, or unfair during an argument?

107.
Is walking away during conflict self-control, or avoidance?

108.
Do our apologies include a plan for change, and do we follow up on how we'll repair the behavior?

109.
Do you think saying "but" in an apology is a way of deflecting responsibility, or can it be a valid explanation?

110.
What does accountability look like to you? And what's the difference between giving context for our behavior and justifying it?

111.
Are there ways power shows up between us in arguments: financially, emotionally, socially, or otherwise?

112.
Are there things that may be "technically allowed" in our relationship, but still hurtful or disrespectful to do?

113.
Are there parts of your partner's life you feel entitled to because you are in a relationship with them?

114.
Is it fair to expect your partner to avoid things that make you insecure, even if they're harmless?

INFIDELITY

115.
Have you ever been cheated on? How did it affect your ability to trust?

116.
Have you ever cheated, even emotionally? What led to it and did you feel guilty or justified in the moment?

117.
Does someone's history of cheating affect whether or not you'd be willing to date them?

118.
If you found out a close friend was cheating on their partner, would you tell them to confess or stay out of it?

119.
Do we believe emotional cheating is as serious as physical cheating—and are we clear on what either of those look like in our relationship?

120.
Are there any behaviors we haven't defined clearly as cheating, and could that ambiguity cause damage down the line?

121.
Do you think flirting counts as cheating? Where do you personally draw the line?

122.
Do you think people who have cheated before are more likely to cheat again? Why or why not?

123.
Do you think monogamy comes naturally to people? And how do you see our relationship—strictly monogamous, or are you open to being poly in the future?

124.
Is there any part of you that believes certain types of cheating is justified or understandable?

125.
If you found out one of your parents had cheated, would it change how you see them?

126.
Do we owe each other full transparency about temptations or close calls, or are there times when withholding something protects the greater good of the relationship?

127.
Is it easier for you to forgive sex without feelings, or feelings without sex?

128.
Is desiring someone else a form of betrayal, or does cheating only start with action?

129.
Do you think I know where the line is between being friendly and being flirtatious—and do you trust me not to cross it?

AFTERMATH & REBUILDING

130.
What do you prefer after a fight: space, affection, reassurance, or something else?

131.
What part of an apology matters most to you: words, tone, timing, or follow-up?

132.
Do you ever feel rushed to move on after a fight? What helps you process at your own pace?

133.
Do you believe people change more through insight or consequences, and how does that belief shape the way you approach forgiveness?

134.
Is there anything you're still carrying from past fights that we've never fully resolved or revisited?

135.
What does it look like for us to meet halfway when a recurring issue keeps causing tension?

136.
Have you ever hurt or disrespected an ex after a breakup? What happened?

137.
Do you think staying friends after a breakup is healthy or confusing?

138.
If we broke up, how would you want us to handle telling people—and how long would you need before it felt okay for either of us to move on publicly?

139.
If we got back together after a breakup, would it matter to you if I had been with someone else in the meantime?

SEX &
ROMANCE

INTRODUCTION

Sex. The elephant in the room. The thing we crave, the thing we neglect, the thing we overthink. Sex is fun. It's hot. It's messy, passionate, awkward, phenomenal, moody, and sometimes just… *blah.*

It has no set pace. It's unique to every couple, and it changes with the seasons of every relationship. It's pleasure. It's primal. And above all, ***it's complicated.***

We've been together throughout our entire twenties. In the beginning, we had sex all the time. Then life happened. We moved in together. Careers, friendships, family… Bigger things took up space. At some point, sex stopped being at the center of our relationship.

Stress slows desire. Exhaustion makes it easy to set aside. And when you're juggling bills and your mind is overwhelmed with responsibilities, sex can start to feel like another task on the list. But sex matters. It's a form of communication: *an opportunity to realign.*

The dynamics of sex in a relationship, just like everything else in a relationship, change. What makes you feel desired, the ways you explore intimacy, even your patterns of arousal. All of it will change.

But the thing that changes the most is the effort you make to have a good sex life. You slip into these norms of seeing the same person every day and feeling like the details are no longer necessary.

The *"**wow, you look beautiful**"* and *"**I can't wait to take you home tonight**"* slowly disappear, as if the effort it took to draw you in is no longer needed to keep you. You stop getting dressed up for date nights. You skip the compliments because at this point, ***she should already know how you feel about her.***

You stop flirting. Anniversaries go from *"**surprise, look where I'm taking you**" to "**babe, our anniversary is coming up—what should we do?**"*

Your appearance becomes less important to you. Maybe even your health does too. Your priorities change. And although these changes are natural—if you don't flag them, they become your new standard. And once this becomes your new standard, routine without effort starts to feel like indifference.

You start confusing being comfortable with not trying. You tell yourself it's fine because you've been together for so long. But the truth is, effort is what keeps your relationship alive. Details matter. The compliments. The effort in your appearance. The gestures, like holding the door and buying flowers. These desires don't just go away once you're locked in.

What goes away is the idea that you still deserve them. As if being in a relationship means you no longer need to feel desired.

You stop expecting things. You stop asking for them. After a while, you forget that desire needs to be maintained. You stop doing the things that make your partner feel wanted. And when this happens, it doesn't matter how much you love each other. Without desire, the relationship starts to feel flat.

•••

Our relationship has had its fair share of rough patches. *Really rough ones.* We've had months where we didn't have sex at all. And not for lack of love or attraction. Just… ***life shit.***

I've had times where the stress and personal stuff I was dealing with just completely wiped out my sex drive. My anxiety would take over, and it felt like my body just shut down. I've struggled with substances too, and that definitely affected things.

The longer we went without being intimate, the more insecure we both became.

And then comes the pressure. ***Like after all this time the sex has to be perfect.*** The pressure makes everything harder. It turns something that should feel natural into something that feels like a test.

You start to overthink it. You wonder if you'll still connect the same way. If it'll feel right, or if it will confirm something you're not ready to process. ***These were some of the hardest times in our relationship.***

Having challenges in your sex life is probably one of the most uncomfortable things to talk about. You don't talk about it with your friends, and sometimes it's even harder to talk about it with each other. It becomes the biggest elephant in the room.

Many couples just settle for it.

•••

We found out the hard way what happens when you stop being intentional with intimacy. And it nearly cost us our relationship. But thanks to some brutally honest conversations and a ton of intentional effort, we were able to get back on track.

Heydee and I still flirt.

We still compliment each other every day. We still maintain our health and our appearance. We cuddle. We make out. We tease each other. Just the other day, we hooked up in the backyard of a large event we were attending. We found ourselves veering off the trail in the middle of the woods to feel a thrill behind some trees. Just cause, ***why not.***

Sometimes, while she's driving, I'll slide my seat back and let my hand slip down my pants. I love what it does to her: the way her jaw tightens. The tension between wanting to watch and needing to keep her eyes on the road.

We take every opportunity to keep things from feeling routine. We chase fun. We are incredibly open to the evolving nature of our intimacy. We explore things. And even after all these years, we're still really satisfied with our sex life.

This isn't because we have everything figured out or because we don't go through stuff. It's simply because we're still willing to put in the effort to make it work.

We still want to impress each other.

•••

I have curiosity and effort to thank for the discovery of most of my kinks. A few years ago, Heydee got into pole dancing, so I bought her a pole and set up a mirror so she could see herself the way I do.

Ironically though, the pole wasn't used to master the art of pole dancing, but rather as a prop whenever we felt like adding some spice to our sex life.

As you mature, you can find your desires changing without ever having the opportunity to discover what they actually are.

But when you keep putting effort into your relationship and stay open to new experiences, you often reveal desires you didn't realize were there—like watching your girl play with herself while she's cuffed to a pole, staring at herself in the mirror.

•••

Good sex can't be faked—not really. You have to try things. You have to listen. You have to unlearn what you thought mattered and pay attention to what actually does.

You have to learn how to read a breath. To recognize the change in their body when you've hit the right spot. To play on the edge between teasing and taking. Every kiss along their jawline, every slow drag of your tongue down their neck. Every pause when your lips almost meet theirs, but don't.

These moments of deliberate seduction: **they matter.** They are the heat before the spark. The tease that keeps you hungry. The intentional choices you make to turn a moment that might feel routine into one that feels risky.

The difference between an average night and an unforgettable one is in the details. **Here are some of them:**

What mood does the lighting create?

Lighting sets the mood. Soft, warm light helps you relax and feel less self-conscious. It adds shadows and contrast that make bodies look more defined, drawing attention to what turns you on. We have Hue lights all throughout our apartment, and honestly, they're everything. They set the vibe, and every color combo is visually magnetic. If I could recommend one thing to add to your home, it's **LED lights.**

•••

What does the room smell like?

Scent is often the first thing you notice when you enter a room. Scent is linked to arousal: it activates the part of the brain connected to memory and attraction.

Scents like jasmine, ylang-ylang, and patchouli have been used for centuries to initiate seduction. And don't sleep on the power of layering scents. Lighting a candle with a single spray of your go-to perfume can be incredibly seductive. Even something as simple as misting your favorite fragrance on your pillowcase or adding a few drops of essential oil to the sheets can completely change the experience.

Hygiene:

First things first: fresh breath is non-negotiable. ***But natural body odor?*** That can be a turn-on. Some people love sweaty, messy sex. The scent of your partner after a long day? **Hot.**

Others prefer to shower first. Some are into hairy chests, stubbly legs... everything wild and free. Others go for smooth or trimmed. Grooming is personal.

What matters most is that you feel sexy and confident. Everyone has different needs and comfort levels when it comes to hygiene. Strong smells or textures can be overwhelming for some, while others prefer them. That's why communication matters.

•••

Are you having sex in silence?

Music sets the mood. Especially if it's been a while since you've been intimate, music can make the moment feel less intimidating or awkward. It can also boost your confidence.

We keep a shared sex playlist, and I highly recommend having one. Whether it's slow and sensual or full-on freak mode, your playlist becomes a subtle way to say, *"I'm in the mood."*

Who's making the first move, and do you both like it that way?

Sometimes, what's most preferred is simply knowing. Our brains crave anticipation, not confusion. If you're both silently waiting for the other to initiate, you might end up cuddling... with tension instead of what you actually want. Some people love taking the lead. Others love being pursued. Some spend their lives being dominant, only to crave submission as they get older. And just because you've played one role doesn't mean you can't explore the other. For example, even though I'm the more ***'masc'*** one in our relationship, I still like being dominated.

We enjoy different power dynamics depending on our mood, and we both feel comfortable initiating because we're not worried about being denied without a thoughtful reason. That doesn't mean we're always on the same page. Sometimes one of us is in the mood while the other isn't, but when this happens, it's met with consideration—there's an explanation, and usually a follow-up in the near future.

•••

How comfortable are you with using toys?

Sex toys can be a game changer. Some couples discover all-new kinds of pleasure through toys. Others realize they don't need them, but still like having them as an option. The first time I bought a strap, I was sooo nervous walking into the store.

And funny enough, the sex shop was hosting a class. Literally a group of people sitting in a circle right in the middle of the store. I was mortified, but it was too late to turn back.

I assumed a strap was one piece. I didn't know the harness and the dildo were sold separately. I stood there for at least ten minutes, ***just staring at a wall full of dicks.*** Eventually I just decided to be brutally honest with the store employee and admit I had no idea what I was doing. She was so nice and helpful, and I could tell she appreciated the honesty. What started as an anxiety spiral turned into a funny story I still laugh about.

We used the strap for a few years. Now, it only comes out maybe once a year, if that. Our favorite toy these days is a vibrator we call ***our girlfriend.***

•••

Every element of your environment holds the potential to elevate intimacy. Pay attention to the temperature of the room, the textures against your skin, and the scents around you. These details draw the line between a neutral setting and one that feels erotic.

There's no ***'one way'*** or ***'right way'*** to have sex or to experience intimacy. What matters most is that it feels good, feels mutual, and feels like you. Explore your desires, check in often, and be willing to meet each other where you are—not where you think you're supposed to be.

Limits & Desires

Insecurities & Trauma

Communication & Health

Intimacy & Understanding

Threesomes

LIMITS & DESIRES

140.
How would you describe our current dynamic in bed, who takes the lead more, and is there anything you'd change?

141.
Have you ever been curious about something sexually but kept it to yourself out of fear I might judge you?

142.
How do you feel about switching roles or exploring different power dynamics during sex?

143.
How do you feel about porn in our relationship, whether I watch it alone or with you?

144.
Are there any sexual activities or experiences that you consider off-limits for us?

145.
Are there any specific kinks or fetishes that interest you? Be as specific as you want.

146.
Are you interested in attending play parties? If so, would you prefer to go just for entertainment or to participate?

147.
What's our relationship like when it comes to using toys or accessories, and are you satisfied?

148.
Is there anything you enjoy during sex that you want me to focus on more?

149.
If you struggle with body dysphoria, is there anything you'd like me to do differently that would help you feel more comfortable or confident?

150.
Do you ever feel like your pleasure takes a backseat to mine? If so, has it affected how much you enjoy or initiate sex?

151.
Is there any part of your body you'd rather I avoid during sex, and would you feel comfortable telling me why?

152.
Are there parts of sex that feel performative for you—like you're playing a role instead of being fully present, and where do you think that pressure comes from?

153.
How does your gender identity affect what feels good during sex?

154.
How do you feel about using gender-affirming tools such as packers, binders, or prosthetics during intimacy?

INSECURITIES & TRAUMA

155.
How long could we go without having sex before you start feeling unsure or insecure about our relationship?

156.
When was the last time your body didn't respond the way you expected during sex, and how did you handle it?

157.
Are there moments when you feel disconnected during intimacy? What might help you feel more present and connected?

158.
If I ever pulled away during sex without warning, would your first reaction be worry, rejection, or anger?

159.
Are there any cultural or societal beliefs that influence your views on sex and intimacy?

160.
Do you have any sexual trauma or PTSD that you feel comfortable sharing with me?

161.
Is there anything about sex that makes you feel vulnerable or exposed, including certain words, actions, or tones that might trigger you?

162.
Is there anything I say or do as a joke that actually makes you feel insecure?

163.
Are there ways you protect yourself in this relationship that I might mistake for disinterest or distance?

164.
Have you ever felt like sex was being used as a form of control in a relationship?

COMMUNICATION & HEALTH

165.
Do you feel like we've gotten a little lazy about nurturing our sex life? And do you feel like we're both doing our part to keep it alive and healthy?

166.
Do you think your self-care habits *(diet, exercise, sleep)* affect our intimacy?

167.
Describe our sex life in three words.

168.
Are there unspoken expectations we have about each other's health, hygiene, or habits—and are they fair?

169.
If you've ever felt pain or discomfort during sex, would you feel comfortable sharing that with me?

170.

Do you feel entitled to know if I've ever had an STD, even if I no longer have it?

171.

Do you have a doctor you trust, and how comfortable do you feel being open with them about sexual health concerns?

172.

How would you feel if I gently suggested you visit a doctor after noticing something unusual during intimacy? And how do you feel about regular sexual health checkups as a couple?

173.

How do medications, birth control, hormones, or mental health treatments affect your libido or intimacy—and how openly do you want to talk about that?

INTIMACY & UNDERSTANDING

174.
How often would you ideally like us to have sex?

175.
Aside from sex, are you happy with how physically intimate we are? *(kissing, cuddling, holding hands, etc.)*

176.
Is there anything you'd want more or less of when it comes to physical affection?

177.
What are your thoughts on scheduling sex versus letting it happen spontaneously?

178.
How do you feel about initiating sex? Do you think we both contribute equally?

179.
Can you name three things I do to you during intimacy that really turn you on?

180.
Before sex, what do you require for yourself *(like grooming, showering, or having fresh breath)* to feel comfortable and confident, and what do you expect from your partner?

181.
Are there certain times of day or situations where you feel most in the mood for intimacy?

182.
How comfortable are you talking about masturbation? And do you see it as a solo thing or something that can be part of our shared intimacy?

183.
Have you ever felt weird or guilty about masturbating while in a relationship?

184.
Do you think either of us have used *"that's just how I am"* as an excuse to avoid improving something that's affecting our intimacy?

185.
Do you like dirty talk—and is there a specific kind that actually gets you off versus one that just feels awkward?

186.
If I whispered something dirty to you in public, would it turn you on—or would it make you uncomfortable?

187.
If we were watching something with a sex scene and I initiated intimacy with you during or afterward, would that turn you on or make you uncomfortable?

188.
If our sex life was exactly the same five years from now, would that feel okay to you—or would you feel stuck?

THREESOMES

189.
Have you ever had a threesome? If so, what was that experience like for you?

190.
Would you ever want to have a threesome with me, and if so, how often?

191.
Do you prefer finding a third person through a dating app or meeting someone organically?

192.
Do you have a preference for finding a third locally, or do you feel it should only happen when we are out of town?

193.
How do we ensure we are both attracted to someone we want to sleep with?

194.
Do we want to set rules about seeing a third person again, or should it always be a one-time thing?

195.
Have we decided who would take the lead in pursuing a third person, and what would that interaction look like?

196.
Would you ever hook up with a friend or someone from a social group we see often, and how would that change things for us?

197.
If one of us developed feelings for the third person, how would you want to navigate that?

198.
Are there any limitations you want to set on certain sexual dynamics with a third person, such as using toys or avoiding certain intimate acts?

199.
Have we agreed on specific safer sex practices to ensure everyone involved feels comfortable and protected?

200.
Should we set a rule on how much communication we have with a third before and after our interactions to avoid feelings of jealousy or discomfort?

201.
Have we discussed whether we should flirt with a third person together or separately?

202.
How should we handle jealousy or insecurity if we involve a third person? What happens if one of us begins to feel left out or uncomfortable during the experience?

203.
To avoid awkward or uncomfortable moments, should we agree on a safe word or signal to use if one of us feels uneasy?

LOVE
LANGUAGES

INTRODUCTION

Everyone has their own way of showing love. Some give. Some teach. Some hold on tight, while others love by letting go. When I was younger, I did not understand the language of love. I thought love looked like it did in movies: grand gestures and passionate speeches. If it wasn't obvious, it wasn't real. If it did not match what I had imagined, I did not recognize it as love at all.

My love language is teaching. I see my worth in what I can pass down: ***in what I can help someone understand.*** I've always been drawn to sharing what I know. Yet it took me years to understand where that instinct came from—that the people who raised me hadn't just left memories, but also lessons. And ways of thinking. Ways of being. And without knowing it, they defined the way I love.

•••

My dad *(son of an architect)* spent most of my childhood working on our house. When he bought it, it was gutted and torn apart. But nail after nail, year after year, he turned it into a home—the place where my siblings and I grew up.

He poured everything he had into that house. If we wanted to be close to him, we had to meet him where he was: outside, hammer in hand. We helped pour concrete, lift walls, and sand down splinters. He dedicated every weekend to working on a new project.

Whether it was a new shelf or fixing a hole in the wall, he was always building. And he kept building, the same way his father did. As I've gotten older, I've come to understand that this was his way of loving us.

•••

My stepmom, who was my teacher at the time, entered my life during a period where being self-sufficient was the baseline. My dad was struggling with his mental health. Custody was complicated.

Half the time, I lived in my mom's co-living space: a house filled with single moms, hippies, and tech bros. The other half, I lived in a trailer with my dad. Somehow, in the middle of it all, my dad started dating my teacher.

Suddenly, she was the one driving me home and telling me what to do outside of school. At the time, court orders required another adult to be present during visits with my dad, so she stepped in as that adult. Then we moved into her apartment. Fast forward a few years, they're married, and I have three siblings.

As a parental figure, she was strict. Chores every weekend. I'm talking clean-each-tile-in-the-shower-with-a-toothbrush type of strict. I'd wake up two hours before everyone else just to get a head start on Saturday morning, so by Sunday afternoon, I could go play outside with the neighborhood kids.

I spent a lot of my childhood thinking she hated me.

Her parenting style was completely different from anything I had ever experienced. She went from being the person I looked forward to seeing at school to the person I dreaded coming home to. We clashed. ***A lot.***

Every summer, I was sent to a Japanese summer school. At first, I dreaded it—school during summer vacation felt like punishment. I was bullied, and my lack of understanding of the culture left me struggling to keep up. But over time, it began to feel like something I could belong to.

My stepmom raised me with the values of her culture: respect, responsibility, and discipline. In many Asian homes, structure isn't strict. It's a form of care.

You don't talk back. You take your shoes off when you enter a house. You learn to sit with discomfort and earn your rest. She didn't leave much room for rebellion, only expectation. And in that expectation, I learned what it means to work hard. At the time, it felt like pressure. Now I know it was preparation.

Her love language was discipline. Every lesson was meant to prepare me for a world she knew would be unforgiving. And in her own way, she was right. Life wasn't going to give me special treatment.

My mother, on the other hand, had almost no rules.

She took me to Burning Man when I was 14. We skipped school to follow bird tracks on the road. If I wanted something, I had to write a contract proposing an even exchange. If I had a question, I was not given an answer. I was handed an encyclopedia. She raised me to see everything as an opportunity to learn something.

As a kid, I resented her for it. I saw my friends' parents shower them with affection, and I wondered why mine did not. Their love looked soft. Effortless. Easy to receive. My mother's love looked like *lessons.*

This same approach extended beyond me. It's how she processed everything, including my dad. When he struggled with his health, when they got divorced, she compartmentalized her emotions. She grounded herself in understanding the why, using reason to keep emotion from taking over.

She never burdened me with their conflict. She didn't vilify him or ask me to choose sides. Instead, she turned it into something I could understand. A lesson. She taught me that people are complicated.

That hurt and love can exist in the same space. That sometimes you have to hold two truths at once.

She bought every book she could find on psychology and trauma. What felt chaotic and painful at the time became something else. It became understanding. It became my ability to empathize. To see beyond my own experiences. To recognize that people are not just what they do, but why they do it.

My mom loves by teaching.

She believes knowledge is the way forward. That answers are not something you are given, but something you find for yourself. She never hands me easy truths. She puts the lessons in front of me and lets me figure out what to do with them. It's how she was raised. It's what she knows.

Later in life, I spent a lot of time with my grandad, an immigrant from ***Ramallah, Palestine.*** His entire fate depended on the little pieces of knowledge he could gather despite the chaos around him. The bits of English he picked up from the people occupying his homeland. The survival skills passed down from our ancestors. And the lessons that carried him from being shot by the IDF and left to die in the desert, to college in Egypt, to the life he built for himself in America.

For my grandad, learning was the only guarantee. The only thing that could not be taken. It was about control in a world that offered him none. The right piece of information at the right time could mean the difference between life and death.

When survival was on the line, feelings took a backseat to the choices that kept him alive. He did not have the privilege of leading with emotion, so he led with knowledge.

This truth shaped the way he raised my mother, and in turn, the way she raised me. Now as an adult, the lessons feel less complicated and more obvious.

People love in the ways they were taught.

This realization changed everything for me. It restructured my relationships. And it made me more intentional with Heydee: not just in how I love her, but in how I receive the ways she loves me.

Love comes in several different forms. Some express it through food. Some through gifts or acts of service. If your partner loves through acts of service, acknowledge the effort behind it. If they love through words, listen with the same energy they put into speaking them.

Feelings can come easy, but showing them the right way takes effort. Love isn't one-size-fits-all. To truly connect, you have to recognize the language the other person speaks and be willing to meet them there. And by doing so, you bridge the gap between loving someone and them knowing they are loved.

Understanding Love Languages

Quality Time

Words Of Affirmation

Acts Of Service

Physical Touch

Receiving Gifts

UNDERSTANDING LOVE LANGUAGES

204.
The five love languages are Words of Affirmation, Acts of Service, Receiving Gifts, Quality Time, and Physical Touch. Which of these makes you feel the most loved?

205.
What is your primary love language?

206.
Are there other love languages that resonate with you, even if they aren't your primary one?

207.
Do you think you give love differently than you like to receive it?

208.
Can you recall a moment when I showed you love in a way that surprised you? What love language did that speak to?

209.
Is there a love language that feels overwhelming to you, like physical touch or words of affirmation? If so, what about it feels like too much?

210.
How do you respond when someone doesn't notice the love you're trying to give—do you shut down or try harder?

211.
Do you think love languages apply to non-romantic relationships, like friendships or family?

212.
How would you feel if I showed more of my love language to friends and family, and would that be something you'd see as a red flag?

213.
How do you think our cultural backgrounds or past experiences influence our love languages?

QUALITY TIME

214.
When you picture our ideal quality time together, what does that look like? What are we doing?

215.
How much uninterrupted time do you feel is necessary to spend with your partner each week to feel connected?

216.
How do you feel about regular date nights, and how often do you think we should go out?

217.
Are there any activities, like grocery shopping, cooking, or cleaning, that one of us usually does alone that we could do together as quality time?

218.
Is quality time about what we're doing—or how present we are while doing it?

219.
When you think about your ideal partner, how important is it that they take initiative with things like planning dates and making reservations—and is that something you'd want more from me?

220.
Do you think we're ever too exhausted from work or stress to give each other the kind of time and attention we both deserve?

221.
Can you remember the last time I planned something for just us, without you having to hint or remind me?

222.
If we could only spend one uninterrupted hour together each week, how would you want to use it?

223.
Is there an activity we've never done together that you'd love to try? Would you be up for taking a class or learning something new with me?

WORDS OF AFFIRMATION

224.
Do you feel like I give you enough compliments or say the kinds of things you need to hear?

225.
What kinds of compliments stick with you the most—about your looks, your effort, or your accomplishments?

226.
Is there a part of you that needs reassurance more than you let on? What would that reassurance sound like coming from me?

227.
What are the subtle ways you test whether I still care about you? And do you wish I picked up on them more?

228.
Are there things I say that unintentionally make you feel overlooked or unappreciated?

229.
How do you feel when I compliment you in front of others? Does it make you feel loved or uncomfortable?

230.
What words of affirmation did your younger self need to hear the most—and who did you need to hear them from?

231.
How do you think gender, culture, or past relationships have shaped the way you give or receive verbal affection?

232.
Is it fair to expect a partner to express love in ways that don't come naturally to them? Why or why not?

ACTS OF SERVICE

233.
Is there a specific act of service that would instantly brighten your day or significantly improve your mood?

234.
If I could magically take one annoying or stressful thing off your plate this week, what would it be?

235.
What small acts of service go unnoticed in our relationship, and how can we better appreciate them?

236.
How do you feel when I do something for you without asking? Do you appreciate it, or do you prefer to be consulted first?

237.
What's one thing you'll always go out of your way to do for someone you love—and why that, specifically?

238.
Is there a part of you that fears asking for help or support in our relationship? Where do you think that fear comes from?

239.
Do you ever feel like you're doing more than me in this relationship, not emotionally but practically? Like you're carrying the daily load while I'm just cruising?

240.
Have you ever found yourself keeping score of who does more in a relationship?

241.
Have you ever felt like you were slowly turning into someone's caretaker more than their partner?

242.
How do you typically respond to people doing things for you—do you feel loved, grateful, uncomfortable, or like you owe them something?

243.
How do you want your partner to recognize and respond to the effort you put in?

244.
Did you grow up learning that needing help was a weakness, and if so, do you struggle to accept care from others now?

245.
When you help others, do you expect appreciation or are you okay if it goes unnoticed?

246.
Has anyone ever tried to help you in a way that felt more controlling than supportive?

247.
Can you remember a time you really needed someone to show up for you—and they didn't? What kind of support were you hoping for?

PHYSICAL TOUCH

248.
Outside of intimacy, which types of physical touch (holding hands, cuddling etc) are most meaningful to you?

249.
Is physical touch an important way you feel reassured in a relationship?

250.
Do you feel like you can be honest with me when you don't want physical affection, without it turning into an issue?

251.
What physical ritual could we create, like a handshake or kiss that symbolizes "I love you" just for us?

252.
Is there a part of your body you wish I touched more?

253.
How do you feel about physical affection in public? Where do you draw the line between sweet and too much?

254.
Has past trauma shaped how you experience physical touch, and does it still affect our intimacy now?

255.
When you're feeling overwhelmed, how does physical touch feel to you? Does it feel comforting, or does it feel intrusive?

256.
Are there types of touch that instantly make you uncomfortable or on edge, even if it's from someone you trust?

257.
Have you ever felt like I used intimacy as a distraction from talking about something important between us?

RECEIVING GIFTS

258.
Is gift-giving important to you in a relationship? And what makes a gift meaningful to you—the item itself, the thought behind it, the price, or the timing?

259.
Do you associate gifts with love, obligation, or apology? How has that affected how you give and receive gifts?

260.
Would you describe yourself as a sentimental or materialistic gift giver?

261.
Do you think your partner should know you well enough to pick the "right" gift without asking?

262.
Have you ever received a gift that made you question how well someone really knows you?

263.
Have I ever given you a gift that felt more about what I wanted to give than what you actually needed or wanted?

264.
Are there small, thoughtful gifts you wish I'd give you more often, like flowers, handwritten notes, or your favorite snack?

265.
How would you feel if I wanted to set a spending limit on gifts—would that feel like a boundary being crossed?

266.
How present was gift-giving in your past relationships, and how has that influenced what you expect in your relationship now?

267.
Have you ever felt like someone used gifts to make themselves look good while mistreating you privately?

PERSONAL
SPACE

INTRODUCTION

I didn't have my own room until I was 18, when my mom and I moved to Jersey to live with someone she was talking to at the time. I was so excited. I painted the whole room burgundy, set up a huge mirror, and lined up all my makeup along its edge. It felt like the first thing that was actually mine. But even in my own room, my space wasn't really mine. The guy had a daughter around my age, and honestly, I had a hard time connecting with her.

She seemed to take everything for granted: two parents who had the resources and were willing to give her anything she wanted. And up until that moment, I had never coexisted so closely with someone who complained so freely to their parents. Watching her roll her eyes and fuss about everything really bothered me.

In my culture, disrespecting your parents isn't normal. So while her behavior might have been typical in America, it was shocking to me. It felt like everything I'd been taught about family, rules, and respect suddenly meant nothing.

At first things were cordial between us, but our differences led to a ton of arguments. We disagreed on nearly everything. And without the grace to make room for those differences, conflict became constant.

She felt entitled to my things and to my space. I was always working, and while I was out she'd go through my stuff and help herself: my bathroom products, my makeup... *like everything.*

She also spoke to me in a way that reminded me of the bullies from my childhood. Like this one time she said the reason I didn't have my driver's license was because *'my mom couldn't afford to buy me a car.'* It was really triggering. We were constantly bickering. And every time it would turn into a fight.

My mom was always terrified I'd lose it one day and snap at her out of anger. And to be honest, I wanted to—but I didn't. It was her house, not mine. And I knew drama with her would only make things harder for my mom, who was already walking on eggshells in that relationship.

Looking back at it now, I know I had my part in it. I wasn't always good at giving her space either. I had to learn to adjust to her boundaries too. I had to be careful not to overstep and to notice how the dynamic shifted whenever my mom and I spoke Farsi, which left her out of the conversation. It wasn't one-sided; we both had blind spots.

Living together tested both of us in ways we weren't prepared for. And that experience taught me a lot about what personal space meant to me.

When I met Samantha, she was living in a 5-bedroom apartment in Brooklyn with 6 roommates, but she still had her sanctuary: her room. It was colorful, trippy, and extremely organized. She genuinely loved spending time by herself. Like, loved it.

She'd have projects going and sit behind her screen for hours. And every few months, she'd drop some LSD and do a full deep clean like it was a spiritual ritual. That space was her reset button. I loved that for her, and I wanted that for myself.

I moved out at 22 and into an apartment in Bushwick with three roommates. The dynamic worked well, and I was grateful to finally have my own space. A year later, Samantha and I decided to move in together.

About a year after that, the pandemic hit.

When Covid hit, my life changed overnight. I was laid off almost immediately, as massage therapy was one of the first fields to get shut down. Suddenly the career I had built was gone, and we were scrambling to figure out what to do. We needed to make money, and, well… New York City needed to get stoned.

Fast forward a few months, and through some creative pivoting, we managed to keep the bills paid.

But living together, working together *(even getting our periods at the same time)*, and never being apart eventually caught up to us. Being together 24/7 meant every thought and feeling had an audience. There was no time to process on my own. If I was upset, Samantha was right there when it happened, there while I was working through it, and there when I finally got over it. She saw every stage, even the parts I was still trying to understand myself.

Being two girls meant we noticed everything.

Every micro-aggression was clocked. After a while, it started to feel like there was no boundary between my emotions and hers. If I was anxious, she felt it. If she was frustrated, I absorbed it. Everything was shared in real time, and that level of closeness *(while beautiful in some ways)* was also exhausting.

Personal space isn't just physical. It's also emotional capacity. It's giving your partner the time it takes for them to think. It's knowing when to give them time to decompress or process before you try to fix things or ask for an explanation.

During Covid, space was something we just didn't have. So we had to start making intentional choices about it. That meant saying yes to separate plans, hanging out in different rooms, and being willing to adjust our mindset. It took a lot of patience *(and more than a few fights)* to figure it out.

We practiced not taking things so personally. We started giving each other grace instead of attitude. We became more patient with each other's moods. We gave each other permission to have alone time without guilt. We found little routines that helped us recharge on our own. And we figured out how to share a home without feeling like we were sharing every thought.

•••

Personal space is also about someone's literal space: as in the way they need their environment to feel.

It took a lot of understanding and awareness to cope with each other's need for particular adjustments. I used to get frustrated when I'd come home and see that she had rearranged all of our furniture. But as I got to know her over the years, it became clear that moving things around was therapeutic for her. She was stress cleaning.

And while the gym is my way of decompressing, rearranging and deep cleaning random things in our apartment is hers.

Now, I appreciate it. I don't fight her on it. And I know that if I don't like anything, she'll happily move everything back. For her, it's not about needing things a particular way—it's more about the act of changing something. The process itself is what helps her.

Thankfully, we both love decorating. We love making our space a reflection of both of us. She smiles when she finds ways to include my decor, and I love seeing her family's things sitting next to mine.

Your space should be your sanctuary. It should make you happy and make you feel good. You should treat your space like you treat your relationship and each other... like it's worth investing in.

•••

Personal space is what allows you both to exist outside your relationship. It's what lets you keep your hobbies, your goals, and your weird little interests alive. It's what keeps you from losing sight of who you are on your own. When we tried to do everything together, we were actually missing out on the quality time it takes to nurture those individual parts of ourselves.

At some point we were like... *wait, we've been so wrapped up in each other that we forgot about ourselves.*

Now, we still spend time together, but it's more intentional. If I want to watch TV, she doesn't have to. If she wants to be on her computer for hours, cool. If she wants to go to bed early, that's fine. I'm a night owl anyway, and she's a morning person.

A relationship shouldn't require you to give up the things that make you, you. The most sustainable ones make room for both togetherness and independence. Long-term love takes two people who can stand alone and still stand together.

That's the only way it works.

Time Management

Privacy & Proximity

Recharging & Comfort Levels

TIME MANAGEMENT

268.
How much alone time do you realistically need in a week to feel grounded and clear-headed?

269.
Have you ever felt pressured to join me for social plans even when you didn't want to?

270.
Does the way we manage our time leave enough room for things outside of us—like time with friends or hobbies?

271.
Is there something you miss doing alone but haven't said because you think I'd take it the wrong way?

272.
What's a sign that one of us isn't getting enough personal space?

273.
Have you ever felt like I rely on your presence for things I could do alone?

274.
Does the way I manage my time make you feel like you're not a priority—even if it's because of work or obligations?

275.
Do you ever pull away or seem busy when you really just need space? What makes it hard to ask for it directly?

276.
Have you ever felt like you had to cut back on your hobbies, friends, or time for yourself to make room for 'us'?

277.
When I leave the house, what's your guilty pleasure solo routine you immediately jump into?

PRIVACY & PROXIMITY

278.
How do you define privacy in a relationship, and do you think we've respected each other's boundaries?

279.
Is there a difference between secrecy and privacy?

280.
Are there specific actions or behaviors you consider a violation of trust or privacy?

281.
What's the best way for me to ask for privacy when I need it, without making you feel like I'm shutting you out or excluding you from my life?

282.
What are your thoughts on sharing passwords and access to personal devices like phones and computers or location?

283.
Can you think of a time when I crossed a boundary or invaded your privacy, but you didn't say anything because you wanted to avoid conflict?

284.
How would you feel if you caught me snooping through your things?

285.
Has there ever been a time I said something about you to others that made you feel uncomfortable?

286.
Have you ever felt like our friends are too involved in our relationship?

287.
Growing up, how much privacy were you given, and how does that influence what you need now in a relationship?

RECHARGING & COMFORT LEVELS

288.
What activities or routines help you recharge and unwind when you need alone time? And are there any that matter so much to you, you'd feel upset if I intruded on them?

289.
When you're emotionally or physically drained, do I make things easier for you—or harder?

290.
Do you ever feel like you have to defend your way of relaxing—like it's not 'productive' or 'good enough'?

291.
When you say you need space, do you actually mean *"don't talk to me"* or just *"don't need me right now"*?

292.
Have you ever skipped something that helps you recharge *(like creative time or a walk)* just to avoid tension with me?

293.
Are there moments when you wish I'd take the hint and give you space—without you having to explain it to me?

294.
Is there a specific time of day you need to recharge, and do we want to set boundaries around being interrupted during that time?

295.
Do you need silence to focus, or are you okay with background noise and talking while working?

296.
When one of us is working, what actually counts as an "*interruption*" to you?

297.
Do you feel like working from home has blurred our boundaries between work time and together time?

TRAUMA & ABUSE

INTRODUCTION

Abuse isn't necessarily obvious. Sometimes it hides in the way someone withholds affection, dismisses your emotions, or twists reality until you no longer trust yourself. It can be subtle or it can be violent, but either way, it has an impact.

Humans are complicated. Some of the kindest people I've known have also caused the most harm. Some of the most abusive people I've encountered have had moments of compassion that made me question my memory.

Abuse doesn't require a villain, only someone incapable of holding their own pain without passing it on. Nobody is born a monster. Sometimes it comes from people who are hurting, people who mean well, or people who love you.

That's what makes abuse so hard to name. When someone hurts you and then cries in your arms after, it creates confusion. Your brain holds two conflicting truths at once: ***they hurt me and they love me.*** And the more you try to make sense of it, the more you minimize your needs. You rationalize your pain. You treat the good moments like proof that it isn't all bad, even if that proof is the very thing keeping you stuck.

There's a term for this: **trauma bonding.**

It happens when abuse is mixed with moments of affection. Your nervous system starts to associate the person hurting you with the feeling of relief that follows.

That's why healing often begins long after the abuse ends: when you finally have distance. Because as long as your body thinks it's still in danger, it prioritizes survival over reflection. It's only when you're no longer bracing for impact that your brain can start making sense of what actually happened.

•••

Abuse is often misunderstood as something just physical.

Something that can be reported or *proven.* But some of the most damaging abuse is verbal, precisely because it's intangible, and because it rewires your inner monologue in someone else's voice.

Verbal abuse is repetition with negative intention.

It's being told you're too sensitive, too emotional, or too much, until you internalize the criticism and police your own emotions. It's the slow distortion of your self-perception, masked as sarcasm, feedback, or ***I'm just being honest.*** And perhaps the most dangerous thing about verbal abuse is how easily it hides inside the relationships we defend.

You get used to being mischaracterized and misunderstood, until one day you find yourself defending your abuser to protect the logic you've built your world around.

•••

Abuse can turn you into someone you don't recognize. You might mirror the harm you received. You might become reactive, cold or manipulative. And you might not notice it right away, because when you grow up in dysfunction, certain behaviors don't feel wrong. They feel normal.

This is one of the many reasons addressing abuse is so difficult. It requires you to admit things you may feel shame around. Like admitting that you've been hurt. Or admitting that you've hurt someone else. But self-awareness is a responsibility to yourself. It's the difference between repeating a cycle and breaking it.

Whether you are working to unlearn harmful behaviors or figuring out how to respond differently after experiencing them, the responsibility to manage it is yours.

•••

I grew up in a household where, let's just say… communication wasn't our strong suit. Things often escalated. Yelling was the norm. Cops were called. The whole 9 yards. Sometimes, when it got really bad, my siblings and I would go stay with the neighbors while things cooled off.

As I've gotten older, I've had to confront how toxic behaviors from my adolescence stayed with me. Like the words that come out when I'm angry or the way I react when I feel cornered.

Even the way I've handled other people's pain. At times, I've struggled to offer empathy when someone's challenges seemed small compared to what I'd lived through. But I've learned that pain isn't meant to be measured.

I don't blame my childhood for my behavior or for my decisions. But I see how much it influenced me, and how easy it is to repeat what you see. I still have a lot of work to do, but I've come a long way. I hold myself accountable. I learn from my mistakes. And as difficult as it may be, when Heydee checks me on my bullshit, I listen—and I prove it by changing how I behave.

•••

Abuse is never excusable. Not under stress, or in the heat of the moment. Abuse remains unacceptable in every context. It isn't justified by having a bad day, feeling overwhelmed, or being insecure in a relationship. It also isn't excusable just because it happened to you. None of these reasons make it okay to belittle, control, or harm someone else.

In the queer community, harmful behaviors can sometimes go unrecognized as abuse due to stereotypes or misconceptions, but that doesn't make them okay.

Abuse in LGBTQ+ relationships isn't less violent, less damaging, or more forgivable simply because it defies the heteronormative script.

Still, the reality of relationships, especially long-standing ones, is ***complicated AF.*** While some behaviors are never okay, not every moment of harm signals a pattern of abuse. Human beings are flawed, and relationships inevitably involve conflict, rupture, and repair.

A mistake, if it's owned and followed by real change, is different from ongoing abuse. The key is knowing the difference without minimizing the harm.

•••

Abuse comes in many forms. It lives in the homes of people you'd never expect, and in the lives of people who seem fine. Even the happiest people you know may be experiencing it behind closed doors. That's why it matters to check in on your friends, to ask again when your gut tells you something is off, and to never stay silent just because the truth might make things uncomfortable.

I know this not only from my own experience, but from seeing it happen to people I love. Every time, I've wished I'd known what was really going on sooner. I pray my loved ones always feel safe enough to tell me. That they know I'll meet them with love, not judgment. Because the truth is, the less judged someone feels, the safer you become in their eyes.

And safety always matters more than opinions.

•••

If abuse is part of your reality right now, please know this: **The number of times you've left or gone back doesn't erase your right to safety or your right to something better.**

It doesn't matter how many times you swore you'd leave, or how many times someone stepped in to help. It doesn't matter if you had choices and made the wrong ones.

Choosing to love someone, or give them another chance, never means you agreed to be hurt. Nobody deserves to be harmed, no matter the circumstances.

I know how heavy the shame can feel, how quick the voice in your head is to say, ***"you did this to yourself."*** But that's self-blame talking, **not reality.** You are not a burden. And you're not too far gone to be worth saving. Your voice matters. Your life matters. And you will ***always*** be worth it.

Awareness & Accountability

Thoughts On Therapy

Addressing Trauma

AWARENESS & ACCOUNTABILITY

298.
How do you define abuse in a relationship—whether it's physical, emotional, or mental?

299.
Do you think abuse can show up in ways that aren't loud or aggressive—like guilt-tripping or emotional manipulation?

300.
Are there any behaviors you once thought were normal in relationships but later realized were abusive?

301.
What personal boundaries do you find most important to establish and uphold to prevent abuse in a relationship?

302.
What specific things tend to trigger you, and can you share why they have that effect?

303.
Do you think you're capable of recognizing and acknowledging behaviors in yourself that might be abusive, even if they're unintentional?

304.
If someone called your relationship "toxic," how would you know whether it was projection—or something worth taking seriously?

305.
How comfortable are you admitting that you were wrong or apologizing when you hurt someone?

306.
If harmful behavior arises in our relationship, would you be willing to seek help even if it means sharing our business with someone else?

307.
If you ever noticed me treating someone in my life in a way that felt harmful or abusive, would you feel comfortable bringing it up with me?

308.
If someone told you they were experiencing abuse, how do you think you would respond?

309.
If we ever put hands on each other, could you imagine any situation where forgiveness would still feel possible? Why or why not?

310.
Have you ever felt the need to constantly *"explain"* your partner to others because their behavior made people uncomfortable?

311.
Has there ever been a time you felt intimidated by me—physically, emotionally, or mentally?

312.
Are there ways I might unknowingly mirror someone from your past who hurt you, and how can we navigate that?

THOUGHTS ON THERAPY

313.
Have you ever tried therapy? What was that experience like for you?

314.
Is there anything you've learned in therapy that you think would help us communicate better?

315.
What are your thoughts on individual vs. couples therapy?

316.
How do you feel about us attending therapy as a preventative measure, even when things seem stable?

317.
If I want therapy for our challenges but you prefer privacy, how can we find a compromise that works for both of us?

318.
Have you ever had a negative experience with therapy, and how did it shape your views on seeking help in the future?

319.
Has any part of you avoided therapy because you fear being misunderstood or *"diagnosed"*?

320.
When choosing a therapist, what qualities matter most to you? Would things like being queer, trans, or a person of color make a difference in how comfortable or seen you feel?

321.
Do you worry that therapy could make you realize things about this relationship you've tried to ignore?

322.
How would you respond if our therapist said your behavior was at the root of our biggest struggles?

ADDRESSING TRAUMA

323.
What's the most painful or traumatic experience you've been through that you're willing to share with me?

324.
Are there topics or situations that feel off-limits for you right now because of past trauma? If so, how can I respect those boundaries when they come up?

325.
Do you ever fear that your trauma makes you *"too much"* for another person to handle?

326.
Have you ever shared your trauma with someone and regretted it? If so, what happened?

327.
Are there coping strategies you used to survive past trauma that now feel unhelpful or even harmful?

328.
How do you define self-sabotage, and have you noticed it in either of us? If you saw me doing it, would you feel okay calling it out?

329.
Have I ever triggered you in a way that brought up past trauma, but you didn't feel comfortable telling me?

330.
What's the difference for you between feeling supported and feeling like someone's trying to fix you?

331.
If we run into someone from your past who caused you harm, how can I best support you in handling any anxiety or discomfort?

332.
Is there anyone who has hurt or abused you in the past who is still part of your life?

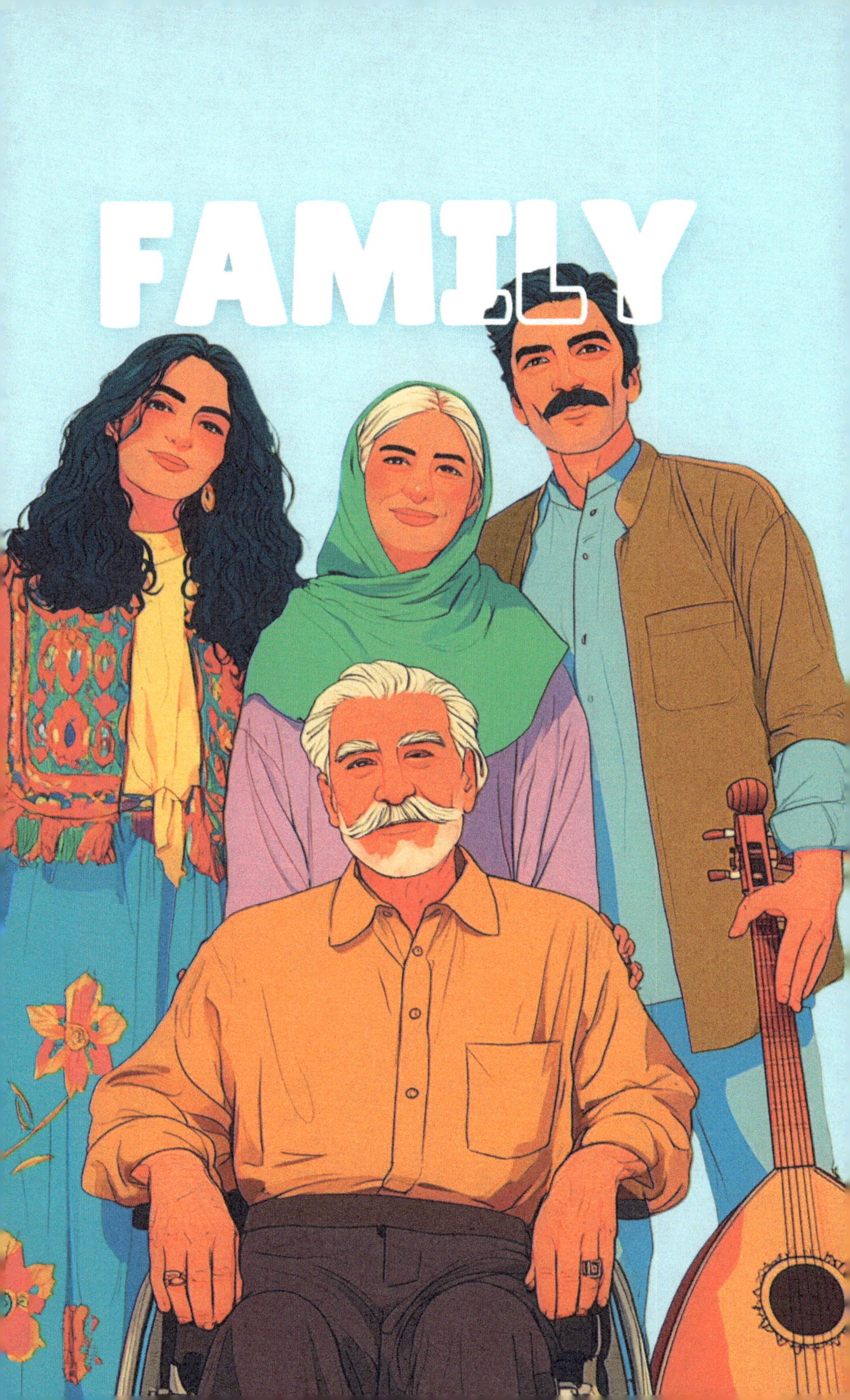
FAMILY

INTRODUCTION

Family has always been the floor beneath my feet. I grew up with a solid sense of feeling loved, not only from my relatives, but from everyone around me. Where I'm from, that kind of warmth was the baseline. And it shaped what I came to understand as normal.

Community is the heart of my culture, influencing everything from daily life to generational traditions. We celebrate in circles. We grieve in crowds. The idea of being ***on your own*** doesn't land the same. People don't wait to be invited into your joy or your pain. Involvement is instinct, not intrusion. Iran is a country built on collective resilience and tight-knit family structures. It's the neighbor who brings food when someone is sick. The cousin who helps raise your kids. The friend who becomes your sibling. Individualism takes a back seat to family, and it's common for relatives to live together or stay close by.

I grew up in ***Shiraz, Iran,*** packed into a house full of people. Grandma. Aunts. Uncles. Cousins. Some of my best memories are from back home. I remember my grandmother waking up at five in the morning to start the *Ghormeh Sabzi.* The whole house would fill with the smell before the sun was even up. She would tell me to set up the *Sofreh.* In the afternoons, we'd sit outside in the garden—snacking on dates, sipping saffron tea. We had the biggest walnut tree in the neighborhood, and my grandmother made sure anyone who stopped by went home with a handful.

Moving to America was a shock to my system. Parents and kids lived separately. Affection was expressed in more reserved ways. Family ties felt looser, more distant. What felt ordinary back home felt almost impossible to find in the U.S.

I spent much of my time in America missing the comfort of my family. But when I met Samantha, something felt familiar. She understood things I didn't have to explain. She was the first person I dated who truly grasped how much my culture and traditions mean to me, and she has always made sure to honor that.

Although we come from different upbringings, our cultural habits overlap in a way that celebrates us both. Even the items passed down from our families, tucked on shelves and hung on walls, fit together in a way that feels natural. When I ask her three times if she's hungry, she doesn't get annoyed—she smiles, because her mom does the same thing. I know her holidays, and she knows mine. She asks about my family, and her siblings are my siblings.

•••

It's easy to connect over what's familiar. What matters more is how you handle what isn't. There are parts of my life that exist side by side but rarely overlap. I'm not out to my relatives in Iran. I filter what I share. I keep parts of my life separate. But none of that means I'm any less proud of who I am.

When you're in a cross-cultural relationship, some questions don't have clear answers. Marriage matters. Visiting my home country matters. Being able to bring my partner with me matters. But these things can't necessarily exist at the same time.

Traditions, laws, safety, timing: ***they all matter.*** Some situations don't have a solution. Sometimes, you're just standing between two things that are equally real, equally important, and equally complicated. In these moments, the right partner will sit with complexity, support without pressure, and honor what isn't theirs to change.

Samantha has never made me feel like I had to choose between my family and my relationship. She sees how much my family means to me. And vice versa. Her family comes with its own complexities, and I would never put her in a position where our relationship came at the cost of that dynamic. My family is complicated, and so is hers. We don't pretend to have the same experiences, but we make the effort to understand each other's context. And we respect what matters to each other, even when it looks different from what we know.

Not all families hug. Or talk. Some check in constantly. Some disappear when it matters most. Some are warm, expressive, and always around. Some are distant, cautious, or turbulent. People can love you and still not understand you. They can support parts of you and reject others. They can mean well and still cause harm. Some keep their distance to stay sane.

Others stay close because walking away costs too much. And for many, it's seen as less of a choice and more of a duty. Culture, survival, history—it all ties in.

You may look at your partner's relationship with their family and not understand it. You might think they're too loyal, too forgiving, or too willing to adjust. But love doesn't always follow logic. People stay connected to their families for reasons that won't always make sense to you. Maybe they're afraid of what will happen if they finally speak up. Maybe they still crave approval they've never gotten. Maybe they worry about losing access to siblings. Or about who will take care of a parent when they get older.

Maybe they've been taught their whole life that turning your back on family isn't an option.

These choices aren't always about love. You might not agree with how they handle it. You might think they deserve better. But it's not your place to decide how they should navigate their past. You didn't grow up in their shoes. You don't carry their history.

In the end, the goal isn't to fix their family. It's to stand beside them as they navigate what that relationship looks like. To support the version of family they choose to carry forward. And to build something of your own that feels solid, even when the foundation you started from wasn't.

Coming Out & Acceptance

Conflict & Boundaries

Family Dynamics

Support & Traditions

Family Roots & Stories

Life With Pets

COMING OUT & ACCEPTANCE

333.
Who was the first person you came out to, and what were your biggest fears about how they would react?

334.
Do you think it's possible to live an open and proud life without being out to everyone? Are there people you've chosen not to come out to—and why?

335.
Do you have any family members who identify as LGBTQ+? If so, what's your relationship with them like?

336.
Has anyone in your family ever confided in you about their sexuality or identity before sharing it with others?

337.
Has anyone in your family used religion, culture, or 'values' to justify rejecting you?

338.
Is there anyone in your life that you've stopped speaking to because of how they responded to your gender identity or sexuality? What happened?

339.
How do you reconcile loving family members who may not fully accept your LGBTQ+ identity? *(If applicable.)*

340.
If a family member asked you to "not talk about it" around certain relatives or at certain events, would you comply?

341.
How open do you want us to be about our relationship in public, especially around people we don't know well or in places where we might not be fully accepted?

342.
How would you feel if your partner introduced you as a friend or a roommate to someone they haven't come out to yet—or to avoid making a situation uncomfortable?

CONFLICT & BOUNDARIES

343.
How would you describe your relationship with your family right now, and where would you rank the importance of family in your life?

344.
What behavior from family do you refuse to tolerate?

345.
What does loyalty mean to you when your partner and your family are in conflict?

346.
How should we respond if someone from our family shows disrespect toward our relationship?

347.
Do you believe it's ever possible to repair a relationship with a family member after serious hurt or betrayal?

348.
If one of us feels uncomfortable visiting a family member due to past conflicts, what approach would feel right for us?

349.
If I chose not to have a relationship with your parents or family members due to conflict, how do you think that would affect our relationship?

350.
What kind of behavior or boundary-crossing from a parent or family member would be serious enough for you to consider distancing yourself or ending the relationship with them?

351.
How would it make you feel if a family member invited me to something (like a trip, wedding, or birthday) but asked that I come without you?

352.
Can you recall a time when you were the one who escalated a family conflict? What triggered that reaction?

353.
How do you feel about me stepping in when you're having a tough conversation with a family member? Do you want me to offer support or give you space?

354.
If I notice behavior from your family that feels emotionally abusive, how would you want me to handle that conversation with you?

355.
If I ever get into a heated argument with one of your family members, will you stand up for me, even if you don't fully agree with me?

356.
Has a conflict with your family ever pushed you to your breaking point or triggered a mental health crisis?

357.
What's a boundary you've successfully set with family, and what helped you hold it?

FAMILY DYNAMICS

358.
Have we fully intertwined our families, and are we happy with where things stand between our families right now?

359.
How involved do we want our families to be in our relationship and everyday life?

360.
Do you feel more like a child or an adult when you're around your family—and why?

361.
How would you feel if one of our parents moved in temporarily?

362.
How do you feel when a family member oversteps by giving unsolicited advice about our finances or how we run our home?

363.
Is there anything about how I was raised or my relationship with my family that you've ever questioned but didn't feel comfortable bringing up?

364.
Have you ever wished I had a better relationship with your family?

365.
What did your upbringing teach you about love or loyalty that you still carry with you today?

366.
Have you ever felt like you had to "manage" your family when I was around?

367.
Do you believe there's a limit to how much we should sacrifice financially for family?

SUPPORT & TRADITIONS

368.
What's a family tradition or memory that means a lot to you, and why?

369.
What traditions or values from our families do we want to incorporate into our own relationship?

370.
Are there any traditions or family events that are important to you to be part of, like weddings, graduations, or major milestones?

371.
Were there any traditions from your upbringing that you disliked?

372.
Do you have any ideas for new traditions we could start together?

373.
How do we want to celebrate holidays—especially if our families have different traditions or beliefs?

374.
If your partner didn't want to participate in one of your family's long-standing traditions, would you respect that or expect them to go along with it anyway?

375.
Do you feel like I respect and encourage you to honor and uphold your culture and traditions?

376.
Are there people in your life who feel more like family than your relatives? What earned that role?

377.
How can we support each other if we feel torn between obligations to our biological family & our chosen family?

FAMILY ROOTS & STORIES

378.
Can you share a family event or trauma that still affects your family today? How do you think it shaped the way your family communicates or deals with challenges?

379.
Is there someone in your family you feel really connected to? What makes that bond special?

380.
Can you recall a time when a family member made a sacrifice for the good of your family?

381.
Has there ever been a family member who you feel was misunderstood or unfairly judged?

382.
Is there a family member who had a significant impact on the person you've become?

383.
What stories and lessons from your elders do you feel responsible for passing down?

384.
What's a childhood memory you rarely talk about, but that really stuck with you?

385.
Can you tell me about a time when your family's expectations felt too heavy on you, and how you managed that pressure?

386.
What's a pattern in your family that you've noticed repeating over generations, whether it's a behavior, belief, or communication style?

387.
How do you typically process grief, and what kind of support do you need from me during difficult times?

LIFE WITH PETS

388.
Do you want pets? How do you see pets fitting into your future: non-negotiable, nice-to-have, or situational?

389.
Is there a specific pet you'd like to get someday?

390.
Are you willing to compromise on getting a pet if one of us wants one but the other doesn't?

391.
If I have a pet, would you feel comfortable helping me care for it if we moved in together?

392.
Who do you think should be responsible for the day-to-day care of a pet—like feeding, walking, or cleaning up?

393.
What is your financial limit for pet care, such as vet visits, grooming, or training, and how do you feel about budgeting for these expenses?

394.
Do you think pets should be allowed on furniture or in certain areas of the home, like the bed or couch?

395.
If we get pets, do we have a plan for who can take care of them when we're away?

396.
Do you think the partner with fewer responsibilities or a more flexible schedule should take on more of the pet care? Why or why not?

397.
What role did pets play in your childhood, and how does that influence how you feel about having them today?

KIDS

INTRODUCTION

To have a child, whether you raise one, teach one, or simply love one, is to participate in a time loop. You're witnessing the future while being haunted by the past. Their wonder reminds you of everything you've forgotten. Their questions surface things you've buried. They make you answer questions you stopped asking. *Why is the sky blue? Why do we lie? What happens when we die?* They make you explain rules you follow automatically. *Why do we shake hands? Why can't we eat dessert first?*

We spend years teaching kids how to follow rules. How to sit still. How to behave. We rarely stop to ask what they're teaching us: how to forgive quickly, how to be fully present. How to find joy in the smallest, most overlooked things. Like puddles. *And bugs.* They love without conditions. They fall, cry, and try again without shame. Their entire existence is built on curiosity and courage.

Then we start this process we call **socialization.** We teach them to moderate themselves. To moderate their tone, their joy, their sadness, and their curiosity. We reward compliance and call it maturity. And as kids grow older, they learn to detach from their most vital instincts. In the name of preparing them for the world, we often strip them of the very qualities that might heal it.

Yet, despite this pruning: they love us. They forgive us. They wake up every day ready to try again.

Their capacity to hold wonder, to be present, to feel without filter is a form of genius we rarely acknowledge. It's resilience in its purest form.

I'm the oldest of four, with all three of my siblings at least eight years younger. Some of my earliest memories are of taking care of kids. If I wasn't home with my siblings, I was helping my stepmom at work look after other people's children. I got a front-row seat to the reality of raising kids: the exhaustion, the cost, the endless demands. It takes months before they sleep through the night. Diapers burn through your paycheck. Formula, wipes, bottles—clothes they outgrow in weeks. Creams and medicines you don't think about until the moment you need them.

Then there's the crying. The desperate, inconsolable wailing when they're sick for the first time. When their gums are raw from teething. When they're overwhelmed by a world they know so little of.

Every parent knows that feeling: *the helplessness of cycling through solutions, hoping something finally works.*

I've lived close to the reality of parenting. Close enough to admire it. Close enough to be afraid of it. And close enough to question whether I want it for myself. I know it's not a simple decision. But honestly, I love the idea of being a parent—and so does Heydee.

We talk about it often, and hope it's an option for us one day. Not just possible, but sustainable. We want to raise children without having to dismantle the life we've worked so hard to build.

We are raised in a culture that treats parenthood as inevitable. It's baked into our fairy tales and our timelines. We're taught to see having children as a milestone. But being queer interrupts this narrative. We're not handed a script for family. We have to write our own. For queer parents, nothing is assumed. There's no *oops,* no accident. Parenthood, for many LGBTQ+ couples, requires intention, and often, a staggering amount of effort. Surrogacy, IVF, adoption, fostering. Every path to parenthood is layered with legal hurdles, financial strain, and emotional vulnerability.

It can cost tens of thousands of dollars. And even then, success isn't guaranteed. For many queer people, the question isn't whether I want to be a parent, but *whether I can afford to try.* And still, so many of us do. We fight bureaucracies. We piece together support. We build families anyway. **That's love with a backbone.** A refusal to let systems define what we're allowed to hold. And a commitment to love, even in the face of structural resistance.

•••

Not everyone who parents is recognized as one. There are people performing the hard, daily labor of raising a child: nurturing their sense of safety, shaping their worldview, and offering stability where none existed.

Yet, they are treated as secondary. Foster parents are seen as placeholders. Gay parents are asked whose biology the child belongs to. Trans parents have their very identity framed as a liability. We've been taught to think of parenthood as something defined by genetics and legality. But those markers don't always reflect who's doing the work. They reflect who's been allowed to claim the title.

Parenting is an act. A set of behaviors that show up across roles and relationships. It's in the way someone reaches out an arm at a crosswalk when a child steps too close to the curb, or the way a tired cashier makes a toddler laugh while scanning groceries.

You don't have to share blood to feel responsible for the next generation. You don't have to carry a child to carry a sense of duty.

At its core, parenting is an instinct. An urge to protect those who can't protect themselves. To pass on what you've learned. It's a commitment to leave the world a little better than you found it: not just for your own kids, but for ***all kids.***

We tend to think of being a parent as black and white: you either are one or you're not. And while that may be true in many ways, I believe parenthood is more fluid than that. I think it lives in the choices we make on behalf of those who don't have a choice. I see parenting as a torch we carry together, each of us taking a turn, even briefly—to light the path for someone coming next.

Thoughts On Parenthood

Parenting Approaches

Co-Parenting

Navigating Family

Challenges & Bullying

Identity & Diversity

THOUGHTS ON PARENTHOOD

398.
How do you feel about having kids? Would it be a dealbreaker if one of us wanted them and the other didn't?

399.
What qualities do you see in us that you believe would make us great parents? Be specific.

400.
What would be your preferred path to having kids (adoption, IVF, surrogacy, or something else)? And how would you feel if we didn't agree on the same route?

401.
What's your biggest fear about becoming a parent, and how do you think we can address it together?

402.
How do you envision dividing parenting responsibilities (childcare, homework, discipline, and chores)?

403.
Have we talked about how we'd afford having a child—like looking into jobs that offer fertility, adoption, or surrogacy benefits, or starting a savings plan?

404.
When thinking about potential donors, do factors like race, ethnicity, or cultural background influence your decision? Why or why not?

405.
What values or lessons are most important for you to pass on to our children?

406.
If one of us wanted to give our child significantly more independence while the other preferred to keep stricter boundaries, how would we navigate that difference?

407.
How would you respond if our child pursued something we strongly disagreed with?

PARENTING APPROACHES

408.
How do you feel about disciplining our kids? What approaches or strategies do you believe are most effective?

409.
How do you want to handle situations where one of us makes a decision on the spot that the other disagrees with?

410.
If one of us becomes the "fun" parent and the other the "disciplinarian," how do we keep resentment or imbalance from building up?

411.
How do you feel about our friends/family disciplining our kids, and what boundaries would you set around this?

412.
Until what age do you believe we should financially support our child (high school, college, or beyond)?

413.
At what age do you think kids should start making their own choices about things like clothes, hobbies, or curfews?

414.
How do you plan to handle situations where our child may challenge authority or rebel?

415.
Are you willing to apologize to your child when you're wrong? How would you feel if they called you out or held you accountable?

416.
How much of your approach to parenting is influenced by what you felt was missing in your own childhood?

417.
How do you picture handling tough talks with our kids, like grief, sex, or death?

CO-PARENTING

418.
What does your ideal co-parenting dynamic look like after a separation or divorce?

419.
If my ex and I had a strong co-parenting relationship, would you ever feel uneasy or jealous about the communication between us?

420.
If my child from a past relationship struggled to connect with you, how would you approach that situation?

421.
How involved would you want to be in parenting decisions for a child that isn't biologically yours?

422.
How would you feel if our child confided in one of us more than the other?

423.
How should we handle it if we strongly disagree on a financial decision for our child?

424.
How would you want me to bring it up if I ever felt like I was carrying more of the parenting responsibility?

425.
If one of us went through a mental health crisis, what do you think would be the best way to support our child through it?

426.
If your co-parent started showing signs of addiction or mental health struggles, would you step in early or wait until things got dangerous before considering full custody?

NAVIGATING FAMILY

427.
Should kids be taught to respect all relatives and elders equally?

428.
If I have a family member dealing with mental or substance-related struggles, how do you see us navigating their relationship with our child?

429.
What boundaries should we set with our families when it comes to unsolicited parenting advice?

430.
What role do you think extended family members should play in our children's lives?

431.
If a family member frequently makes negative or rude comments about our child, how would you address this?

432.
If there's a family member you've had a falling out with, how do you feel about our child still having a relationship with them?

433.
How do we handle asking for support from family when we need help, whether it's with childcare, financial assistance, or emotional support?

434.
If our child picked up a harmful belief or behavior from a relative—how would we address it?

435.
If our child prefers spending time with one side of the family, do we let that naturally happen, or do we try to "balance it out" even if it feels forced?

436.
How do we approach a situation where a family member introduces something to our child (like religion, gender roles, or politics) that we've intentionally chosen to hold off on?

CHALLENGES & BULLYING

437.
How would you respond if our child faced bullying or discrimination at school?

438.
If our child was bullying others, how would you address it?

439.
If our child told us about being bullied but didn't want us involved, how would you balance respecting their wishes and ensuring their safety?

440.
If our child expressed thoughts of self-harm, what steps would you take to ensure their safety and well-being?

441.
Would you ever allow our child to confront their bully face-to-face in a controlled setting, or do you think that could cause more harm than good?

442.
If our child feels different, excluded, or rejected, how would you want to help them build confidence—at home and at school?

443.
If our child were being bullied, do you think we'd respond differently? Who do you think would react more emotionally, and who more logically?

444.
If a teacher or school authority dismissed our child's bullying experience, would you be more likely to escalate the situation or take a different approach—and why?

445.
How would you handle it if our child was disrespectful to a teacher or elder?

446.
If our child fought back against a bully and got in trouble—would you defend their actions or push them to resolve conflicts differently?

IDENTITY & DIVERSITY

447.
How would you approach the conversation if our child questions their gender identity or sexual orientation?

448.
How would you feel if our child wanted to change their first or last name to reflect a different part of their identity?

449.
What steps can we take to help our child respect differences in race, culture, and identity, and to ensure they grow up surrounded by diverse role models and communities?

450.
How would you react if our child wanted to adopt religious or political beliefs that completely oppose our own?

451.
Do either of us speak more than one language? If so, how important is it to you that our kids grow up bilingual?

452.
What would accountability look like to you if you found out our child said or did something racist or culturally insensitive?

453.
How would you handle a situation where our child feels disconnected from or rejects their cultural background?

454.
Would you feel fully prepared to raise a child whose racial or cultural background you don't personally share?

455.
How do you imagine explaining our child's donor story to them, and do you feel clear about how much we'd share—and when?

456.
If our child grows up with more privilege than we did, how do we teach them gratitude and humility?

457.
How would you handle it if our child dated someone who didn't respect our identity, values, or family and didn't want a relationship with us?

458.
What role should we play in shaping our child's online presence—are we guides, gatekeepers, or just observers?

459.
If our child wanted to express their sexuality, culture, or political beliefs publicly on social media, how would you feel about it?

460.
How would you handle it if our child posted something online that embarrassed us or challenged our values?

461.
If our child is being targeted or excluded online, how do we support them—and when do we step in?

MARRIAGE

INTRODUCTION

I've always loved the idea of marriage. There is something so beautiful about two people choosing each other, standing side by side, and saying, this is my person.

Marriage has the power to strengthen a relationship, provide legal protections, and offer financial benefits. But at the same time, I have always questioned whether it is truly necessary to legitimize love.

For most of human history, marriage was not about love. It was a transaction. A means of survival. A way to unite families, merge resources, and secure bloodlines. It was about power, property, and sometimes straight-up politics.

The idea of marrying for love is actually ***pretty new.*** It wasn't until the last few centuries that romance entered the picture. Before that, marriage was shaped more by societal needs than personal desires. Women were traded as property. Alliances were brokered through vows. And though marriage has evolved, traces of its history remain in the expectations placed upon it. It's still used to define legitimacy, measure success, and decide what counts as *"real"* commitment.

In Iran, marriage is an expectation.

I can still hear my grandmother asking, *"When are you getting married?"* It was a question I never answered honestly. Instead, I would smile politely and say, *"Maybe one day."* She would nod and give me advice I did not need. *"Find a rich man who will take care of you. Marry him. Start a family."* She was like a second mom to me; we were so close.

Unfortunately, I was never able to share my truth with her. She passed away in late 2024, and it still hurts that she never got to see me walk down the aisle. Not to a rich man, but to someone who truly loves me for who I am. I wish she could have witnessed the version of love I've built for myself: one where freedom and partnership coexist.

Sometimes I feel guilty for never coming out to her. Part of me wonders if she's looking down, hurt that I kept that part of myself secret. In the end, I think she would have wanted me to marry the person I love. I think what mattered to her wasn't the ritual of marriage, but the recognition it brings: the sense that your love is real in the eyes of others, and therefore, **protected.**

Marriage, more than anything, is about recognition. It's a way society acknowledges a partnership as real. It's also a milestone people assume you will reach. And if you don't take that step, the questions follow. The assumptions. *The judgment.* As if love, no matter how genuine, is incomplete without the ceremony to seal it.

Samantha and I have been together for nearly a decade. We've built a life side by side. We've grown together, made sacrifices for one another, and chosen each other through every phase of our relationship. And yet, because we are not married, sometimes I feel like we have more to prove.

I've found myself worried that some people may not take our relationship seriously. That without the ring, others might see us as less committed. It's often the first question people ask: *Why aren't you married?* Or *when are you getting married?* As if it's appropriate to ask something so personal.

I know it's innocent. But it feeds into a deeper, subconscious belief that a strong couple still needs an explanation if they're not married. It reflects the assumption that love only counts when it's legally recognized.

I'm still learning to let go of the judgment *(real and imagined)* and to remind myself that our relationship is not defined by how others perceive it.

If we do get married one day, it will be on our terms. No stress. No financial strain. Right now, our priority is building the life we've always dreamed of: leaving our nine-to-five jobs behind. We want to travel, take care of our families, and eventually build our own. Marriage isn't off the table, but it's not our main focus.

Despite being queer, people continue to expect our relationship to follow heteronormative roles and traditions.

I feel for Samantha sometimes. Because she's seen as the *"masc"* one, people assume she should be the one to propose—as if I don't get a say, or as if being the *"femme"* means I can't ask her first. Honestly, if we had a dollar for every person who's pulled her aside to ask when she's going to propose, we'd be rich by now.

Truthfully, we're all just trying to navigate relationships in a way that feels right, despite the expectations placed on us. And maybe that's the real work: *learning to trust the choices we make, even when they don't fit the timeline society expects.*

•••

From the things I've witnessed in our community to the stories I've heard over the years, I can't help but notice how much we tend to romanticize marriage. We convince ourselves it's the thing that will strengthen our relationship. We dream about the anniversaries and the big ceremony… but ignore the everyday reality that comes after.

Some couples say it's the best thing that ever happened to them, but behind closed doors it can just as easily cause resentment or a sense of being trapped. For many, leaving feels harder than staying.

At the same time, marriage gives queer couples legal and social recognition. It allows partners to sponsor a spouse for visas, be present in medical settings, make healthcare decisions, and build or adopt a family.

And beyond these legal protections, marriage is a moment of joy and affirmation: the chance to stand before family, friends, and the world and say, ***"we choose each other."*** It's a way to honor commitment, and everyone deserves that right.

•••

We grow up being told there's a proper order to life: marriage, then a house, then kids. But that plan was built in another era under circumstances that no longer exist.

Relationships come in all forms, and each one deserves to be recognized and respected.

Some couples marry, some don't, some raise kids, some build lives together without them. The range of possibilities is what defines this era. It's easier than ever to look around and realize you don't have to copy someone else's life to have a good one. The best part of living now is the freedom to move at your own pace and build a life that reflects one *you* truly love.

Timing & Planning

Ceremony & Traditions

Before & After Marriage

TIMING & PLANNING

462.
What are your thoughts on marriage, and is it something you want for yourself?

463.
Is there anything about marriage traditions, vows, or ceremonies that makes you uncomfortable?

464.
If one of us is ready for marriage and the other isn't, how long are you willing to wait before its a dealbreaker?

465.
If we weren't financially or professionally where we wanted to be yet, would you be okay waiting to get married?

466.
Do you think we've assumed who should propose based on tradition, gender roles, or unspoken expectations?

467.
Do you think we should both contribute equally to the wedding expenses, and ideally, what do you think our budget should be?

468.
When it comes to big financial decisions, where does a wedding or getting married fall on your list of priorities?

469.
Do you have any personal goals or dreams you want to achieve before we get married?

470.
Are there specific people who would affect the timing of when you'd want to get married *(for example, family who live far away)?*

471.
What are your top three must-haves or dealbreakers for our wedding *(like no kids, certain traditions, or something else)?*

CEREMONY & TRADITIONS

472.
What does your ideal wedding ceremony look like, and are there any particular traditions or elements you're excited to include?

473.
How can we combine our cultural or religious traditions in our marriage while respecting each other's beliefs?

474.
Do you prefer a large wedding or would you rather have an intimate micro-wedding?

475.
Would you prefer a local wedding or a destination wedding?

476.
If we had to cut costs for the wedding, what would you be willing to let go of, and what would you want to keep?

477.
How would you feel if your family didn't approve of the way we chose to celebrate our marriage, and would you be willing to stand firm in our decision?

478.
If wedding planning begins to strain our relationship, what's the first step you'd want us to take?

479.
Have you ever felt pressured to be excited about marriage and if so, where do you think that pressure came from?

480.
What do you think is more common—marrying the wrong person or marrying at the wrong time? And which one do you feel we've seen more of in people around us?

481.
If we never got married but stayed committed and built a life together, would that feel complete to you—or would you feel like you missed out on something important?

BEFORE & AFTER MARRIAGE

482.
If we start having doubts about getting married at any point, how should we address those feelings?

483.
How do you feel about prenups, and would you be okay signing one?

484.
How do you feel about taking, keeping, or hyphenating last names after marriage?

485.
If our sex life changes after marriage, do you see that as normal—or a red flag?

486.
If you were okay with how I dressed, carried myself, and expressed myself before marriage, do you think you're entitled to have a say in it once we're married?

487.
If we hit a rough patch in our marriage, what's a step we can agree to take before considering separation?

488.
Is there anything you expect to change in how we behave around other people once we're married?

489.
Would it bother you if I didn't want to wear my wedding ring every day?

490.
What concerns or fears do we have about marriage?

491.
Do you think marriage gives us more say in each other's choices, or should our independence stay the same?

492.
Is celebrating anniversaries important to you?

HEALTH & WELLNESS

INTRODUCTION

My mom was diagnosed with stage 2 breast cancer two years after my stepdad died of lung cancer. Losing my stepdad was the first real death I experienced. I had been to funerals before, but the actual concept of dying never really crossed my mind until he got sick.

Cancer is an brutal disease. It turns you into someone weak before it kills you. You lose your strength and your energy. You stop looking like yourself. And those who love you have to sit there and watch it happen. People try to help, but there's nothing anyone can do. You're in pain, and they're in pain, and nobody knows what to say.

Everyone tries their best to keep a positive attitude, but inside, they're just as lost. And somehow, everyone in your circle has to figure out how to talk around the most obvious truth: ***that the person they love is probably going to die.***

We were just starting to get settled down in America when my stepdad got diagnosed with cancer. And he died within a year. When he died, his family came and took ***everything.*** They literally showed up at our apartment and emptied it, as if it was our fault he got sick. Although we lived in America, we didn't fully know our rights, so we let them do whatever they wanted.

At the time, my mom still knew very little English. Most things still felt foreign. And after he died, she had to figure everything out on her own—my school paperwork, her taxes, our rent. We moved into a tiny one-bedroom apartment in Queens. We made it work. I got my first under-the-table job at fourteen, and every dollar I made went toward groceries. That $100 a week made me feel like the man of the house. Then my mom got diagnosed with breast cancer.

Losing my stepdad made cancer very real, so when my mom got diagnosed, I was devastated. I used to sit with her during chemo sessions, trying to bury the dark thoughts in my head. The idea of losing her and being completely alone in America was always in the back of my mind.

There were many times my mom considered going back home. Being a single mother in a foreign country, working two jobs with a daughter and cancer, feels like a nightmare. And it was. But despite the odds, she recovered. My mother is my definition of strength. She's the strongest person I know.

I've lost a lot of people I love to illness and health complications. And over time, I became a little numb to it. Detached, even. I avoided checkups for years. Every time I thought about going, I'd picture the worst-case scenario. I'd rather not know than sit in a room and hear I had something I couldn't fix. And somehow, because life is funny like that, I ended up with someone who is the **exact opposite.**

Samantha has an obsessive fear of illness. She grew up in a house where medicine was hoarded, and the people around her were always on the edge of being sick. Getting sick was used as a scare tactic—like, ***"If you don't do this, you could get sick."*** As she got older, her obsessive patterns just fed into that paranoia. As an adult, it became her default reaction. She'll notice something, Google it, spiral, and book an appointment immediately.

I'm not gonna lie, at first, it annoyed me. Especially because I've spent years trying not to live in constant fear of getting sick. I'd watch how she spiraled over the smallest thing and think, ***Damn, your fears aren't even rational... and you let them take over. Meanwhile, mine are rational. I've seen what illness does. I've watched it happen. And somehow, I still don't let it run my life.***

But eventually, I realized that her anxiety was real—it was just a different version of my own. She ran toward her fears; I ran away from mine. I avoid. She reacts. I shut down. She goes into hyperdrive. Neither approach is perfect, but being together helped us find the middle. And somewhere in the middle, we found balance.

She encouraged me to stay on top of the things I'd avoid. She signed me up for health insurance and helped me book my first Pap smear. Medicaid makes you jump through hoops and sit on hold for hours, but she relentlessly insisted until I was fully covered and had all my checkups booked.

I help her slow down when her mind runs off in ten directions. We balance each other out. We're still learning, but we've gotten better at recognizing when our behaviors are being influenced by our trauma.

Being in a long-term relationship means going through a lot of changes together—physically, emotionally, and hormonally. Since we've been together, our bodies have changed. We've gone through weight gain, weight loss, mental health dips, digestive issues, hormonal imbalances, and the stress of just… *life*.

The pandemic was hard AF on our relationship. Samantha lost weight from stress; I gained it. I ate to calm my nerves. She lost her appetite. Our coping mechanisms were opposite. We were both struggling, just in completely different ways. We had less sex and argued more. We both felt insecure about our bodies and our overall well-being. In other terms, *we fell off.* We had to relearn how to take care of ourselves. And by extension, each other.

That's what love looks like sometimes. Not just cuddles and date nights, but the unglamorous work of helping each other come back to life.

When we stopped prioritizing our health, it nearly ruined our relationship. So we got back to the basics: better food, more movement, drinking water, sleeping at a decent hour.

And as we became more intentional about our health, it showed. We had more energy. We argued less. We felt sharper and more at home in ourselves.

The more we take care of ourselves, the better we are together.

Although I've had a tendency to avoid the doctor, I've always been into wellness. And I've maintained a pretty healthy lifestyle. That's why I became a massage therapist. Becoming a massage therapist helped me understand the body in a more realistic way—how we store stress, how we hold tension, how pain shows up physically when we don't process it emotionally.

I've worked with people from all walks of life—athletes, CEOs, parents, everyday people just trying to feel better. And the one thing they all have in common is this: **Your body always knows.**

Before you admit you're stressed, your sleep gets weird. Before you admit you're upset, your jaw locks. Your posture changes before your mood does. Physical tension is often the first sign something's off.

Tense shoulders? You're bracing for something. *Gut issues that seem random?* Your gut has more nerve endings than your spinal cord, which is why emotional stress often shows up as stomach pain before anything else.

I can't stress enough how important it is to pay attention to what your body is trying to tell you.

Still, even when you are paying attention, your body doesn't always give you clear answers. Even though I put a lot of effort into taking care of myself, I've still faced health challenges—just like so many women do, often undiagnosed or untreated for years. I've dealt with PCOS, and navigating it has been one of the hardest parts of my wellness journey. Unfortunately, even when you prioritize your health, some things are completely out of your control.

•••

I'm not one of those people who thinks you need to be obsessed with your health. I'm not counting every calorie or doing a cleanse every month. But I do pay attention. I know when I'm off. I know when I've been pushing too hard or not moving enough.

I'm intentional with my daily habits. I eat healthy. I work out. And I remind myself that taking care of my health isn't just for me; it's for the people I love.

If you're in a relationship, health and wellness is both personal and shared. Your habits affect your partner, just like theirs affect you. You set the tone for each other. Whether you realize it or not, you build routines together.

If your partner stays up late and eats like shit, chances are you're ***doing it too.***

On the flip side, taking care of yourself can inspire your partner to do the same. Loving someone means pushing each other to be better, even when it's easier to stay the same. It's saying the hard things instead of letting them slide. It's holding each other accountable: not out of judgment, but out of belief in what's possible. And it's trusting them to do the same for you.

Living a *"**healthy life**"* is a way of showing up for yourself, even when it feels like the last thing you have time for. It's a form of gratitude: an awareness that nobody gets to choose the body they're born into, and that if you were blessed with a healthy one, you should appreciate and cherish it.

Most people wait for the *'**right time**'* to change, but that time never comes. **Start where you are.**

Choose one thing that supports your health and keep choosing it until it becomes part of your routine. Start small and stay consistent. Consistency will always beat intensity. Decide that your health matters and let your actions reflect that, one choice at a time.

Wellness & Support

Care & Communication

Physical Health & Fitness

WELLNESS & SUPPORT

493.
How important is health and wellness to you personally?

494.
How do you define a "healthy" relationship with your body and mind?

495.
Do you feel like I support your health goals, and how do you want to be supported if your motivation drops or routines fall apart?

496.
Growing up, how important was health in your family, and how does your upbringing influence your lifestyle today?

497.
How do we prioritize self-care in our daily routines, and are there areas where we can improve?

498.
What's one thing you do every day without fail, no matter what's going on around you?

499.
What's your go-to coping mechanism when you're stressed, and how do you want me to be involved (or not)?

500.
What's a health habit you admire in others but have struggled to adopt yourself?

501.
Are there things I do that you think are harmful to my health—and that you want me to work on?

502.
If I developed a preventable health issue because of my lifestyle, would you feel resentful or obligated to take care of me?

CARE & COMMUNICATION

503.
Do we have any dietary preferences or restrictions to consider, and do our eating habits align overall?

504.
Do either of us take daily medications, and do we support each other in managing or remembering them?

505.
What's our routine around sleep—are we getting enough, and are there habits we could tweak for better rest?

506.
Are we proactive about health screenings *(like pap smears, mammograms, prostate exams, or blood work)*, and do we remind or encourage each other?

507.
Do we know each other's family medical histories, and do we use that information when making decisions about our health?

508.
Does our health insurance cover LGBTQ+ specific care, like hormone therapy, top surgery, or other gender-affirming procedures?

509.
If one of us needed gender-affirming or LGBTQ+ specific medical care, how would we handle insurance, costs, or finding providers?

510.
Do we have our medical info easily accessible (allergies, meds, conditions) in case something happens?

511.
Do we both know where to go in an emergency, and who to contact if one of us can't speak for ourselves?

512.
What's your relationship with substance use and is it for celebration, comfort, habit, escape, or something you haven't fully unpacked yet?

PHYSICAL HEALTH & FITNESS

513.
Where does fitness rank on your list of priorities?

514.
What does movement or exercise look like for you right now—routine, occasional, nonexistent, or evolving?

515.
Do you currently feel confident in your physical strength and stamina or do you feel like you're building (or rebuilding) it?

516.
Are there any past injuries or physical limitations we should be mindful of when planning activities together?

517.
Do you prefer working out alone, with a partner, or in a group? And would you be open to input and guidance from me?

518.
What kind of support around your health actually helps you—and what starts to feel controlling or judgmental?

519.
If I decided to make a big lifestyle change (like cutting sugar, going vegan, or training for a race), what would you do to support me?

520.
What's harder for you: starting a routine or staying consistent?

521.
How do you feel about meal prepping or cooking together for a healthier lifestyle?

522.
If we signed up for a fitness challenge together, who do you think would have an easier time following through with it, and why?

MENTAL HEALTH

INTRODUCTION

Mental health is the state of your mind. It shapes how you think, how you feel, and how you see the world. Your brain weighs about three pounds; inside it, around 86 billion neurons fire signals across tiny gaps called synapses. That firing creates thought, memory, instinct, and emotion.

To understand mental health is to see how unstable it can be; how the line between wellness and illness is often thin and fragile.

I grew up thinking about this stuff. I had to. Mental illness wasn't some far-off idea or soft-spoken secret. It lived in my house. It sat at the dinner table. Proximity made it personal. It taught me that mental illness wears a thousand faces—*often so familiar, you'd never think to question them.*

There are over 200 types of mental illness, each with their own symptoms and triggers; but regardless of the diagnosis, it often begins the same way. It happens when neurotransmitters like dopamine or serotonin fall out of rhythm. It affects everything: mood, memory, and perception.

The brain sends distorted messages, and the body follows.

Sometimes this looks like anxiety or depression. Sometimes it looks like confidence that's too big, beliefs that no one else can see, or patterns that spiral out and never come back around.

Highly intelligent people often make sense of these patterns by finding logic in the chaos and building systems that help them manage everyday life.

This is why the link between brilliance and breakdown shows up so often.

The same drive that pushes people to excel can also push them past their limits. It's not weakness that brings the crash, it's endurance without relief. The mind does what it must to keep going. It bends truth into something livable. But bend it long enough, and it will break.

•••

Mental illness doesn't always look like disorder: it can appear as relentless ambition, exceptional intellect, or moral certainty—even as the mind slips away. And when the mind starts to slip, it doesn't always fall. Sometimes, it rises. It creates purpose. Not every distorted thought is a spiral downward. Some become visions: narratives of importance, or of mission.

The mind reaches for order, and sometimes it finds what it's looking for in God *(or a higher power).*

This is where mental illness meets meaning. Where identity dissolves into prophecy.

The God Complex is real.

It's a psychological state where someone believes they hold special power or authority. It can show up in people who already carry influence, or in those who are trying to reclaim control. Regardless of the source, it creates a version of reality where the person is no longer one of many: they have become the center. The chosen one. The savior.

The God complex *(or messiah complex)* is recognized across cultures. People experiencing psychosis often arrive at sacred sites, fully convinced they are on a divine mission. They speak with clarity and conviction, and reference scripture, myth, and/or prophecy. Some believe they are religious figures, while others believe they have been chosen to deliver a message: one that could alter the course of humanity. The language changes, the location changes, but the belief remains the same.

These patterns are so reliable that they are well documented in clinical psychology. Across cultures and belief systems, the details of the delusion shift to match the world the person knows. But the structure remains unchanged: a grand purpose, a certainty, and a spiritual clarity that feels absolute.

And this phenomenon traces back through centuries of folklore and ritual, embedded in the healing traditions of the ancient world.

In early civilizations, people showing signs of mental struggle were often taken to high places—sacred ground believed to connect humans to the divine. The belief was simple: the gods lived above, and being closer to them might mend what was broken.

But it was not the gods that healed them. ***It was the earth.***

These sites were often near mineral-rich springs. The spring water carried lithium, though no one knew what it was at the time. People would bathe in it and breathe in the mineral-heavy air. Over time, they would return to their communities more like themselves. Today, we know lithium is a mood stabilizer and one of the oldest treatments for psychiatric conditions.

•••

Medication helps.

But meds only work when they are taken. No one can be forced to get help. No one can be made to take the pill or walk into the clinic, even when you love them. Even when you can see the storm before they do.

Free will is a beautiful idea until it collides with suffering. Until it shows up in the middle of a crisis. Until someone you love is spiraling in front of you, and all you can do is watch. Until the person you love is manic, and you have to choose between respecting their choice or saving their life.

And sometimes you can't do either.

•••

I believe in autonomy.

I believe people should have the right to decide what goes into their bodies, how they live, and how they heal. But I have also seen what happens when those choices lead to pain. When someone you love doesn't see their own decline.

I've watched people fall apart while having access to the very thing that could have saved them, and it made me question everything I thought I believed.

There is no answer. Only ***what-ifs.***

What if they had said yes to the meds? What if someone had stepped in earlier? What if I had pushed harder? What if we could go back and try again?

The truth is, no one suffers alone. Mental illness isn't contained to one person's experience. It changes the whole ecosystem around them. Families adjust. Roles reverse. Children become caretakers. Siblings become translators.

Then there's the grief.

A kind of grief no one prepares you for. This isn't the grief of death. It's the grief of absence in the presence of a living body. The person you love changes, and you don't know when or if they'll return. You're still making small talk, still answering their texts, but inside, you're mourning. You're remembering the way their voice used to sound. The way they used to look at you.

Unfortunately, there is no ritual for that. No service. No closure. You live with that grief daily. You feel it in pieces; not all at once, ***but always.***

•••

This chapter almost didn't make it into our book. It would have been easier to write about something resolved. Something I've already worked through. Something I could look back on with clarity and pride, like a finished lesson.

But this isn't that chapter.

My mental health still scares me.

My biggest fear has always been losing my mind. The idea of being the last to know about my own decline has haunted me since I was a child. Maybe that fear is why I take it so seriously.

I am practical about my mental health. I have to be. I maintain structure in my life where I can. I pay attention. I move my body. I get sunlight. I check in with people I trust. I sleep. I eat. I engage in the things I can control, because I know what it feels like to live with the things I can't.

These are small things, but they matter. They add up, and they are choices I make every day in order to stay here.

Yet still, I've had moments where I wasn't sure if I was okay. I've felt emotions that didn't make sense and came on fast: fueling rage I could not reason with. I've had breakdowns. I've watched family members have episodes and have seen pieces of myself in them. I've had months where stability felt like a balancing act.

I've asked myself, *is this just a bad day, or is this the start of something worse? Am I manic?* I've even had phases where I tried to stay ahead of it by numbing everything. I've used downers to keep myself in check, telling myself: *if I never let myself get that angry, maybe I'll never lose control.*

But it only ever brought short-term relief.

What I've learned is that real stability comes from consistency; from showing up for my body every day, even when my mind feels unreliable. And it means accepting that I'll always need to keep tabs on my mental state, not just for me but for the people who love me.

•••

Nearly one in five adults will experience a mental health crisis this year. And when you add a relationship into the mix, things get even more ***complicated.***

Mental health is one of the most common and misunderstood challenges in long-term relationships. From anxiety to suicidal tendencies/ideation, bipolar disorder to schizophrenia—the chances of you or someone you love facing a mental health crisis are **high.**

The best thing you can do is prepare for this reality with radical compassion. Build language around your inner world. Practice communication when things are calm, so you have tools ready when things aren't.

Get curious about each other's coping styles, triggers, and needs. Know your partner well enough to notice the small shifts.

The early signs. The subtle changes in tone or mood that signal something's wrong. Learn how to ask hard questions gently, and learn how to hear the answers without turning away.

•••

Before I wrote this chapter, I spent a lot of time asking myself: *What should this feel like? What should the theme be? What does this information do for the reader?*

For this chapter, the theme was **relatability.**

Not solutions or closure. Just something honest. Something that makes you feel a little more seen. If you take anything from this, I hope it's the comfort of knowing you're not alone. That this kind of struggle is more common than we're ever taught to admit.

And that showing up, even imperfectly, ***still counts.***

General Mental Health

Views & Realities

Support & Self-Care

Suicide & Crisis Support

GENERAL MENTAL HEALTH

523.
Have you ever experienced challenges with mental health, and how did you seek support during those times?

524.
Do ADHD, OCD, bipolar disorder, BPD, or other challenges *(mental health or neurodivergent)* affect your day-to-day?

525.
Are there any specific triggers I should be aware of that could affect your mental health or emotional stability *(like certain topics, actions, or behaviors)?*

526.
Do you have coping tools or strategies that help when you're struggling and how can I help you access them?

527.
Are there any warning signs I should look out for that could be early signs of a mental health crisis?

528.
Do you feel prepared to support me if I were to experience a mental health crisis?

529.
If one of us were hospitalized for mental health reasons, how would we navigate that as a couple?

530.
How do we talk about hurtful things said or done during a mental health episode in a way that holds each other accountable without turning it into guilt, shame, or blame?

531.
Could you be in a long-term relationship with someone who has a mental health condition? What would you need to feel supported and steady in that dynamic?

532.
Would you be willing to attend therapy or learn emotional regulation tools for the sake of your relationship?

VIEWS & REALITIES

533.
What were you taught to believe about people with mental illness growing up?

534.
Do you think society treats mental illness differently than physical illness?

535.
Do you think society romanticizes or demonizes mental health struggles?

536.
Would you feel different about me taking medication for my mental health versus my physical health?

537.
Is there a certain level of functioning someone has to lose before you'd consider them *"mentally ill"*?

538.
How do you feel about the idea of involuntary treatment for mental illness? Should people always have a choice?

539.
How would you want others to respond if you had a mental health crisis?

540.
In your eyes, what's the line between asking for support and being too much? Have you ever worried about crossing it?

541.
Have you ever felt exhausted by someone else's mental health needs and how did you handle that without guilt or resentment?

542.
Have you ever had an outburst or "*crash out,*" and someone labeled you as mentally unwell—even though it felt like a reaction, not a condition?

SUPPORT & SELF-CARE

543.
Are there any mental health conditions that run in your family? Do you ever worry they might show up in you too?

544.
If you grew up with a parent who struggled with their mental health, when did you realize their behavior wasn't *"normal"*?

545.
If a loved one started showing signs of mental illness, what role would you want to take in supporting them?

546.
If a relative refused medication that could stabilize them, would you respect their choice or push harder?

547.
Have you ever had to step in and support a loved one during a difficult moment in public? What did you do?

548.
Do you feel comfortable telling your friends when you're not okay?

549.
What's your limit when it comes to supporting a friend who has mental health challenges—and how do you recognize when you've hit that limit without burning out or ghosting?

550.
Have you ever seen someone use their mental health to avoid accountability? How did you handle it?

551.
Do you think you're more patient with other people's mental health struggles than your own? Why?

552.
Do you think friends or family members struggling with their mental health should always be given grace—or are there moments when they still need to be called out?

SUICIDE & CRISIS SUPPORT

553.
Have you ever experienced suicidal thoughts? If so, what helped you get through them?

554.
Have you ever had a loved one struggle with suicidal thoughts? What did you do in that situation?

555.
Have you ever lost someone to suicide? How did that experience shape your perspective on mental health?

556.
Do you believe suicidal thoughts are always a sign of wanting to die, or can they sometimes be a desire to escape overwhelming pain or circumstances?

557.
If I ever struggled with suicidal thoughts, how would you want me to communicate that to you?

558.
At this stage in our relationship, if you were struggling with suicidal thoughts, would you feel safe telling me?

559.
How would you respond if a close friend confided in you that they were feeling suicidal—but told you not to say anything?

560.
Has a loved one ever used threats of suicide to control or guilt-trip you?

561.
Have you ever assumed someone was exaggerating their pain, only to later realize they were seriously struggling? Did that experience affect the way you respond now when someone says they're struggling?

FINANCES

INTRODUCTION

When we first started dating, I automatically held the door. *Why?* Without saying a word, we both assumed the same thing: I was more masc, so it was my role. No discussion or second thoughts. Just two people subconsciously slipping into the roles we'd seen our whole lives.

I did the *"manly"* things. I built the furniture, took out the trash, and killed the bugs. She cooked, did the laundry, and brought comfort in a way that felt soft and feminine. The irony is, Heydee is more dominant than me. She's direct and unafraid to take charge. But because I wear baggy clothes and prefer topics that *"boys"* are into, I'm seen as the *"man"* in our relationship—while she, the more assertive one, is assumed to be the submissive one.

Despite existing outside the mainstream, queer couples can still internalize and reproduce heteronormative structures.

•••

In the beginning, we both worked minimum-wage jobs. A few years in, I started a business and began making significantly more than her. She was with me every step of the way, yet I rarely included her in financial discussions she had every right to be part of. My self-image as *"the provider"* left no room for outside input. She told me to save money. She told me not to buy stupid shit. ***I did it anyway.*** A few years later, the market became saturated, and my income dropped.

It was time for me to face both a major ego check and a reality check. I had always seen my value in what I could provide—so when I could no longer play that role, I started questioning my self-worth. If I wasn't a provider, *what was I? Who was I?* I felt insecure.

At the same time that my business was falling apart, so were my parents. Both were struggling with their health, and I sent as much money as I could to help. During that time, Heydee took on most of the financial responsibility. She carried us through a period I couldn't handle alone.

Within a few months, I got a job and got back on my feet. For a solid two years, we earned about the same. But with family obligations, I never quite returned to contributing equally.

Then I got laid off.

Getting laid off was gut-wrenching. I was embarrassed, and I felt like I had let everyone down. I kept replaying the moment in my head, wondering what I could have done differently. When your income disappears overnight, so does your sense of control. The future that once felt like a series of possibilities suddenly narrows into one question: *How am I going to make it through this?*

Our brains don't operate at their best under fear.

They cling to what's safe, what's immediate, and what will keep the lights on. Survival mode narrows our vision. We go from building to maintaining, prioritizing what's urgent over what is meaningful. Over time, this kind of pressure blurs the line between burnout and failure.

In these moments, it's easy to compare yourself to people who seem to build freely: people whose minds aren't weighed down by uncertainty.

You start to wonder why you don't have their drive or momentum. But motivation can be a luxury of stability. When survival is on the line, creativity usually doesn't flourish. Urgency takes over. It rewires your brain to focus on the next dollar, the next meal, or the next bill—*not the big picture.*

This is where discipline comes in. Motivation is inconsistent. It depends on energy, mood, and circumstances. Discipline doesn't. It's what gets you out of bed when the stakes are high and your emotions are low. It's not glamorous, but it's reliable. And in survival mode, that reliability can be the difference between staying stuck and moving forward.

Life is chaotic. And honestly, I don't think it gets better. I think we just get better at handling it. I have to constantly remind myself that no one builds something meaningful without setbacks. That every person I admire has hit a wall at some point.

I have had to learn, *and I am still learning*, not to let financial stress seep into places it doesn't belong. To separate my self-worth from my bank account. To resist the instinct to let fear make my world smaller. Instead, I try to focus on the process rather than the outcome.

Getting laid off was what finally pushed me to lock in on this book. That and finding a job, of course. I've been looking for months now, and it's been rough.

Rejection has a way of draining your momentum. You send out resumes and land zero interviews. Before long, you're questioning everything about yourself. But motivation is a feeling. Discipline is a decision. And sometimes, all you've got left is the decision to keep going.

Heydee has been working two jobs for over a year. Then coming home every day to work on this book with me. Our rent is about to go up, and the weight of it all is something we feel every day. Our relationship has taken a toll for this very turbulent time in our lives. I'm sharing this for the sake of honesty. From the outside, we might look all put together. But like every couple, we have our challenges.

Writing this book has forced me to put my thoughts into words: to reflect on my life lessons in real time. In doing so, it's helped me understand them better.

It's given me something to hold onto when doubt creeps in: a reminder that even in moments of uncertainty, I'm still moving forward.

Financial stress doesn't wait for the right time. It finds its way into your conversations, your decisions, and the way you move through life together. Ignoring it doesn't make it go away. You have to face it head-on and talk to one another. ***You have to know where you both stand financially.***

The truth is: **money matters.**

It can make or break a relationship. If you can't afford a stable life, you'll be miserable. If you can't afford to help your family, you'll feel inadequate. If you can't afford to take trips, go on nice dates, or enjoy life together, boredom and resentment will build over time. It doesn't matter how in love you are—if money is tight, stress will follow.

Good news though: if you have internet access, you have access to unlimited knowledge. Skills are free to learn. Information is everywhere. And there are a million ways to make money.

And the best part—you don't have to figure it out alone. You have someone to build, strategize, and move forward with. Take advantage of it. Talk. Plan. Decide. **Apply.**

Financial Transparency

Budgeting & Expenses

Financial Habits & Goals

FINANCIAL TRANSPARENCY

562.
How secure do you feel with money right now, and how much would you need to earn to feel financially stable?

563.
Would you say you're responsible when it comes to saving and spending money?

564.
Do you have a savings account or other investments, such as a 401(k), Roth IRA, or stocks—or would you prefer to keep that private?

565.
How often should we sit down together to review our finances to stay aligned?

566.
Does a partner's income or credit score matter to you, and could either ever be a deal breaker?

567.
What combined yearly income would feel comfortable for us as a couple?

568.
How would you feel If I came into this relationship with significant debt? And how do you think we should prioritize paying off debt versus saving for future goals?

569.
If I were to lose my job, how quickly would you expect me to find a new one, and what kind of support would you be willing to offer during that time?

570.
Would you ever make a money move without telling me *(like a big purchase or investment)*, and in what situation would that feel justified?

571.
Do you financially support anyone besides yourself?

BUDGETING & EXPENSES

572.
Have we set a clear budget for basics like rent, groceries, and daily living costs?

573.
How do you typically approach saving money? Do you set aside a portion of every check, or do you save as you go?

574.
What are your thoughts on both partners going 50/50 in a relationship, and would you be open to that dynamic?

575.
If I earn more, would you be comfortable splitting bills evenly, or should we scale our contributions by income?

576.
Do you check your bank account often, or only when you have to?

577.
When do you think it's the right time to open a joint bank account in a relationship—and would you be open to doing that with me?

578.
Should we set a spending limit for purchases we make without checking in first? If so, what number feels right?

579.
How much should we budget each week for date nights or activities?

580.
Have you ever hidden a purchase because you didn't want to explain it?

581.
When we're creating a budget, how do we decide which expenses are non-negotiable and which ones are more flexible or optional? What happens if we disagree on what counts as a *"need"* versus a *"want"*?

FINANCIAL HABITS & GOALS

582.
When you think about financial freedom, what does that actually look like in your life?

583.
Do you ever feel like you need to *"perform"* a certain lifestyle, and would you feel comfortable telling me if that pressure was hurting your finances?

584.
Have you ever felt pressured to spend money in a way that didn't align with your financial values?

585.
Are there spending habits you've struggled to change, or a purchase you regret that still bothers you?

586.
Do you feel a sense of guilt or anxiety when spending money on yourself?

587.
What's something you currently spend money on that you can't see yourself giving up?

588.
Have you ever felt frustrated or resentful about who pays for what in our relationship, and would you feel comfortable bringing it up?

589.
When it comes to how you spend money, what do you value more—quality or quantity?

590.
Have I ever bought something that made you feel uncomfortable because of the price?

591.
Is there a money habit of mine that makes you think, '*I need to do that too*'?

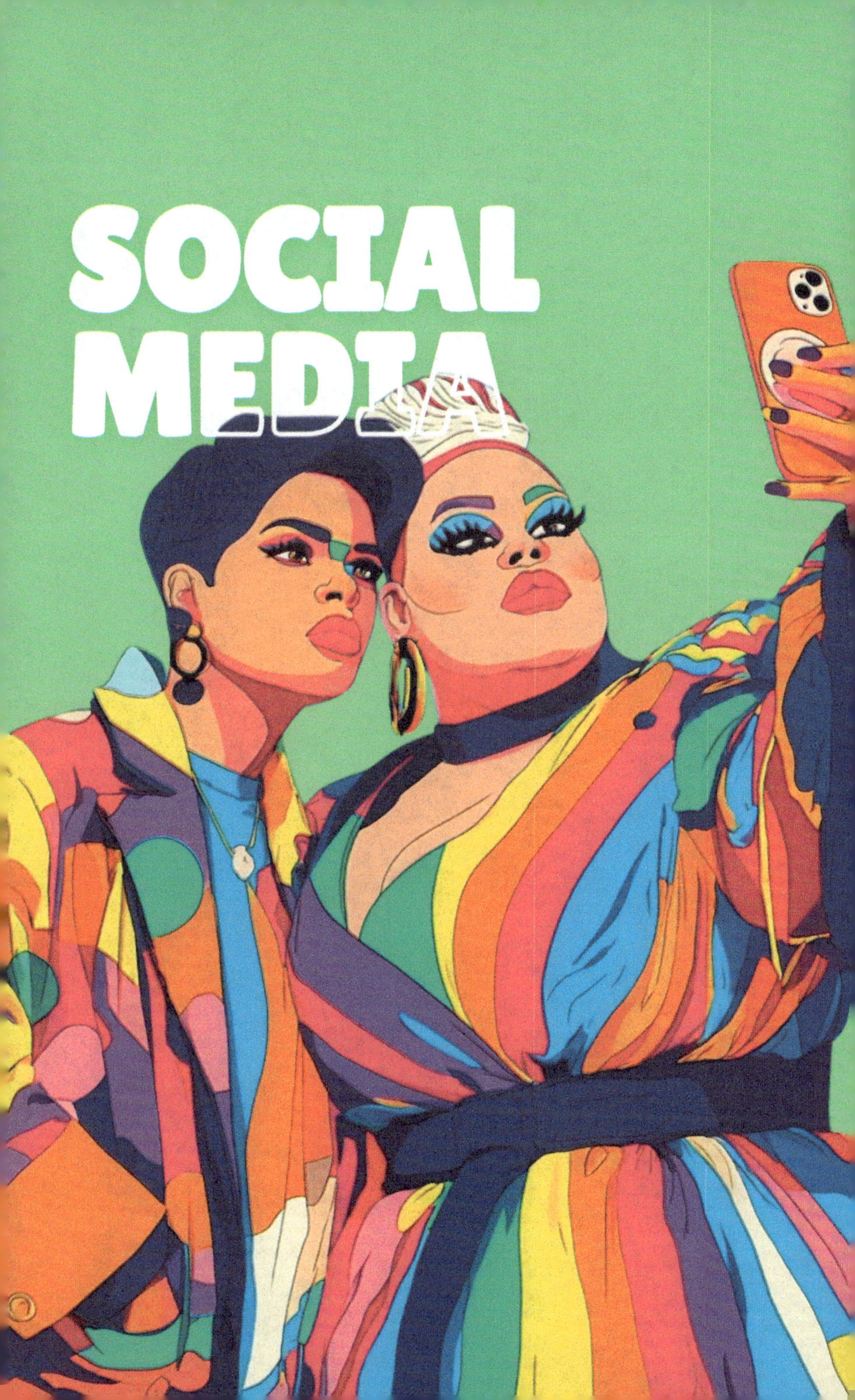
SOCIAL
MEDIA

INTRODUCTION

I didn't come out until I was eighteen. My first girlfriend was older and lived in another state. She slid into my DMs on Instagram back when Tumblr was still a thing.

At the time, I wasn't out. And dating someone across the country felt like a safe way to explore my sexuality with enough distance. ***(Not my best idea.)***

Naturally, we went through each other's comments—scanning for anything suspicious, trying to figure out if there were other girls in each other's lives.

Fast forward a year: I live in New York and we're officially dating. Unlike her, I was freshly out of the closet and still pretty reserved on social media. I'd often feel pressure to post us: a picture at dinner, a photo holding hands.

Not for me, but for her. So she could feel secure. So she didn't feel like I was hiding her. Doing that, though, meant stepping way outside my comfort zone. We broke up for many reasons, but one of them was because of my discomfort with displaying my sexuality online.

At the time, I convinced myself that I was just a private person. It took years for me to realize that wasn't true. I wasn't private. I just wasn't comfortable with my sexuality back then.

It took a while, but eventually I got comfortable with myself on social media. And what I once used to lurk on other lesbians became a way to show my sexuality. The memes I posted, the selfies: they all gave off *more gay.* And now, when I liked a girl's post or slid into her DMs, it was clear I wasn't just being friendly, I was making a move.

•••

Being openly gay on the internet changed how people treated me. Friends I'd known for years admitted they had feelings. I started getting a little more attention online within the LGBTQ+ crowd. And getting that kind of attention made it easier to reach out to people in real life.

I have social media to thank for making my first friends in NYC. I literally DMed a few queers like, *"hey, you seem cool, let's be friends."* And thanks to Instagram, I started building community.

When Heydee and I started dating, I had already been out for a few years, and social media had become part of how I expressed myself. If we were good, I'd post a cute picture of us. If I was upset, I'd post a meme that said what I couldn't. A post that spoke for me—we call this a **sub.**

Social media is built for self-expression, and sometimes that self-expression is a little indirect.

Eventually though, we got better at talking to each other. We agreed that our fights weren't for the internet, and the subs had to stop. Posting a sub might feel validating in the moment, but disagreements aren't meant to have an audience.

Think about it: *if you wouldn't walk up to a stranger in the middle of an argument with your partner and explain your side, why would you do it online*?

Subs create an unfair advantage. They don't talk to your partner, they talk at them—without giving them a chance to respond. What should stay private suddenly feels public, and a small fight can easily turn into entertainment for anyone watching.

As you get older, you start to see subs for what they really are: a cop-out. They don't strengthen communication, they expose the lack of it. A sub says less about your partner and more about your own willingness (*or unwillingness*) to have the real conversation.

Over time, we outgrew subs and replaced them with something stronger: **understanding.**

We learned to understand each other better, like how Heydee calls everyone *"babe"* and I call everyone *"wonderful,"* and neither of us takes it the wrong way.

We also stopped caring as much about how we interacted with others online. When you know where you stand with someone, that kind of stuff just stops mattering. The more we trusted each other, the less we needed constant reassurance.

•••

I could talk about social media all day.

It's fucking fascinating. Ten years ago, companies were paying thirty thousand dollars for TV commercials. Now, one TikTok can influence millions. Couples have gone from venting about their relationships online to making entire careers off them. The landscape of attention has changed, and everyone engages with it differently.

For some, posting a selfie with their partner is a casual way to share joy. For others, it feels like an overwhelming declaration of vulnerability. Some people won't post a relationship until it's serious. Others need to post their relationship to feel like it is.

Social media is an unspoken language and we all speak different dialects.

At its core, social media is attention.

Everything we post. Everything we like or share, it's all about attention. And whether we admit it or not, we all desire it.

This is why jealousy shows up more in relationships now than it used to. Social media puts every interaction on display. Even when nothing is wrong, the constant visibility makes it easier to question your partner's focus.

Social media gives us access to our partner's attention in ways that didn't exist before. And sometimes, seeing that attention directed elsewhere can make you feel jealous or overlooked.

When I post photos of us going out, it's because it feels good to be seen. Yeah, I love taking pictures—but it's also for attention. And once you accept that attention is a basic human desire, you realize it's okay.

You also realize you're not in control of it, *and that's okay too.*

•••

Everyone has a different relationship with social media.

Some people depend on their online presence for income and only post things that fit a curated version of themselves. Others post bikini pictures because they're proud of their bodies and because external validation feels good.

Neither makes them less loyal. Confidence and commitment are not at odds with each other. Someone can celebrate themselves online, attract attention, and still be fully devoted to you.

Love is not limiting someone so you feel secure. It's about trusting that they can live in a world where others see them, admire them, and maybe even want them—without letting that admiration change what you know about their loyalty to you.

And that is just one piece of it.

Social media is complicated. For some, family members don't know they're gay. Others have relatives tagging them in photos they wish didn't exist. People use emojis for all sorts of reasons. Boundaries get confusing and jealousy creeps in. But none of this is impossible to manage. It just means you have to talk about what attention looks like in your relationship, and what does or doesn't feel okay.

You'll both receive attention outside of the relationship—whether you like it or not. It only becomes a problem when it starts to cross boundaries you've already agreed on.

In a healthy relationship, you accept that attention isn't yours to control. And when you recognize that attention is a normal part of life, you also accept that your partner doesn't need you to be their entire universe.

•••

The reality is, you'll never be someone's everything. ***And you shouldn't want to be.***

Honestly, the whole concept makes me roll my eyes. I've always laughed a little when I hear people say that's what they want… to be someone's "everything." ***Like, everything?!***

That's not romance… it's a red flag.

Sure, it sounds cute in a romance novel, ***but in real life?*** No one person should be expected to fill every need you have. I get why it sounds appealing though. We're raised on movies, music, and stories that tell us love means filling every need, being the only source of happiness, validation, and security. But that's not love, that's control.

The truth is, your partner will have needs you can't meet. They'll turn to friends, family, passions, and experiences outside of you, and that's not a threat. It's healthy.

Healthy love means wanting your partner to have a meaningful life, even when it doesn't include you. And in a world where social media keeps us plugged into each other's lives 24/7, that kind of love matters more than ever.

Privacy & Boundaries

Interactions & Insecurities

Shared Social Media

PRIVACY & BOUNDARIES

592.
Do you see your social media account as primarily personal, professional, or a combination of both?

593.
What would you do if you caught me going through your DMs?

594.
Do you think it would be reasonable or acceptable for me to ask for your social media passwords?

595.
What kind of behavior on social media feels supportive to you—and what starts to feel too territorial or controlling?

596.
What do you think about couples sharing their disagreements or conflicts on social media?

597.
Have we set any boundaries around liking or replying to flirtatious comments on social media?

598.
How do you feel about us being on our phones when we're out and spending time together *(e.g., at dinner or when we're with friends)?*

599.
Is there anything you'd want me to ask before posting about you? What parts of our relationship are off-limits for content, even if they'd perform well?

600.
If I posted thirst traps or sexy photos, would it bother you, make you feel proud, or make you uncomfortable?

601.
If I shared a post on social media about something controversial *(like a political or personal stance)* that you disagree with, how would you react?

INTERACTIONS & INSECURITIES

602.
Do you follow any of your exes or past flings on social media? If so, what's your relationship with them now?

603.
If someone from your past slid into your DMs or started engaging with your content, would you tell me or keep it to yourself?

604.
If I met someone on social media who happens to be my type, how would you feel if I wanted to hang out with them?

605.
Have you ever felt embarrassed, jealous, or exposed because of something I posted about us online?

606.
Have you ever felt like our relationship had to look a certain way publicly—even when it didn't feel that way privately?

607.
How do you feel about us following each other's family on social media? Would that change how freely you feel you can be yourself online?

608.
If someone who once hit on me reached out about a work opportunity through social media, would you feel uncomfortable if I took it?

609.
Do you think social media ever amplifies doubts or insecurities in our relationship that we don't talk about?

610.
When we choose to share our relationship online, do you feel like comments from followers come with the territory, or do you take what people say more personally?

611.
If one of us gains significantly more attention or followers than the other, how would that affect our dynamic?

SHARED SOCIAL MEDIA

612.
Do you feel like we both have equal control over our shared accounts and what's posted?

613.
Do we talk openly about how money from social media is split and managed?

614.
If I wanted to step back from being public online, would you support me, even if it came at the expense of our social media engagement?

615.
Do we have a plan for our shared platforms if we ever broke up? And if we did break up, would you feel pressure to fake it online because of money or contracts?

616.
If people attack one of us online, how would you want to handle it?

FRIENDSHIP

INTRODUCTION

Humans are pack animals. We are not built to go through life alone. Long before civilization, before streetlights, before the internet made connection instant and shallow—survival depended on the people beside you. Friendship is the modern echo of this primal truth. It's the warmth around the fire, the reassurance that someone has your back when the world feels too dark or too big to face alone.

Friendship is a paradox.

It's both fragile and unshakable. It's shaped by choice but tested by time. Some friendships last decades, surviving distance and all the ways life stretches us apart. Others slip through the cracks of unanswered texts and good intentions that never made it past the thought. Some end with a fight, but most do not end at all.

They simply stop.

No grand finale or major falling out. No closure. You just stop following up. And before you know it, the person you once called your best friend is a name you hesitate to text.

Yet, even the friendships that fade leave something behind: a version of yourself that only existed in their presence. A set of inside jokes no one else would understand.

One of my best friends got famous at 16.

A few years later, she was *really* famous. People would stop her for pictures. She performed in massive venues. It was wild. She went from having nothing to having the kind of presence that would change the energy in any room she walked into. And because she's naturally generous, she wanted to share it with the people she loved... and she did.

She put us on. Flights, experiences, the wonders of life. She took every opportunity to share the most fascinating things the world has to offer. And to this day, she still does. Most people know her for her talent and her contributions to the music industry, but I know her for her contributions to humanity. For her instinct to give, teach, and question.

I know her as the first to celebrate your wins and the first to tell you when you're selling yourself short. I know her as someone so incredibly dedicated to whatever journey life takes her on. I know her as a wonderful mom who pours her heart into raising, quite literally, the *coole*st kid on the planet. And I know her as someone who, against all odds, has had the strength to not lose herself in a world where so many do.

I've had the same friends for years. Some I've known since we were kids, who I might only talk to once a year, if that. Yet when we do, it feels like no time has passed at all.

I have a friend I met in NYC shortly after I moved here. When we first met, I thought he was a bit weird and drove like a maniac. Fast forward nearly a decade—we've been through the craziest of times, and I'm proud to call him family.

He's the most resourceful person I know, and one of the sweetest. He understands the family dynamics you never really get over: the pain of loving someone who's been changed by demons out of their control. He's someone I know will always understand. We don't talk that often, but I know he'll always pick up when I call.

I have friends who've been dealt some of the worst cards life has to offer, yet they still shine for everyone around them. I also have friends I pray for. Friends I love from a distance. Friends who've given me grace when I've fallen short, forgiven me when I didn't deserve it, and loved me anyway. I have a few friends I've watched grow into adults… ***literally.***

I still remember the day my sister was born. She was all wrapped up in one of those blue and white hospital blankets. We shared a bedroom until I moved to New York. I had the top bunk for pretty much our entire childhood. We're nine years apart.

She probably despised me a little growing up. I was able to escape our chaotic household once I got a car and could dip to my mom's place. I resented her a little too, because she didn't have to clean the bathroom tiles with a toothbrush the way I did as a kid.

By the time our parents had our younger siblings, they were tired. Too tired to be so damn strict. I left for New York shortly after I turned 18. And for years, we barely spoke.

Then one day I came home to visit, and somehow we ended up in the backyard at 2 a.m., talking about God knows what. She was an adult now. And at some point, it clicked for both of us. We are *basically* the same person.

We are incredibly similar. We notice the same details and usually come to the same conclusions. She just gets there twice as fast and three times as gracefully. She's as cool as it gets. And she's the smartest person I know. If I had to pick one person to figure it out *(whatever the fuck it is)* it would be her.

Even though she's my little sister, I'm always learning from her. And not boring shit. Cool stuff. Like stuff about animals and human behavior. She is always teaching me something. I don't think she'll ever fully understand how much I look up to her, but she's always been my compass.

Another one of my closest friends isn't related to me by blood, but he's still someone I consider my brother. I met him when he was still a kid, and I think we all knew he was a star before he did. His light has always been the brightest in the room. He's now become the version of himself he was meant to be, and it's been nothing short of beautiful to watch him step into his potential.

To follow his dreams. To wear the shoes we all knew he would grow into.

I have friends I'll forever be thankful for. Friends who show their love through little details and ridiculously thoughtful gifts. I can't wait for the day I get to return the favor. I look forward to giving them even half of what they've given me.

And then there's Ed. My soul twin. My bestfriend. The person I have to thank for so much of my confidence and growth. Anyone lucky enough to call him a friend knows he sets the bar for what friendship should be. He follows up, and always follows through.

I've probably spent more time with him than with anyone else in my life. We share a lot of the same demons. He's seen me at my best and my worst, and I've seen him at his. We've started businesses together. Ended chapters together. And started new ones. He's insanely clever and one of the few who can keep up with my ADHD brain.

He has this way of making even the messiest situations feel manageable, like somehow we'll figure it out because we always do. He's the first person I call when life blows up, and the first person I want to send a funny meme to. He's the friend who will call me out, call me in, and still call me family. A real blessing in my life. Every year on his birthday, I thank his mom for the gift she brought into this world.

I was lucky. I grew up with incredible friends. What we had in common were the jokes we cracked and the morals we carried. Our sense of what was right... and what was fun. We were the kids who had no rules. Our families were so preoccupied with their own shit, we just kinda roamed free.

We shared an understanding of our own independence: that we were responsible for ourselves. We got jobs early. We shared everything: clothes, gas money, meals. Even a bed at times. Our adolescence was spent at bando parties and in my 1992 BMW that I managed to get for free because it was basically totaled. Somehow, years later, we all managed to get out of the Bay Area and move across the country.

•••

Having famous friends is weird.

You know them in this really deep, personal way: your memories, your inside jokes. All the shit you've been through. And then they walk on stage or into a room full of people, and suddenly they become a product instead of a person.

People act different. They speak in compliments and questions. They want things: Access. Attention. Clout. You see the way your friends slip into the version of themselves the room expects. And it looks exhausting, so you make sure to protect the version of them that doesn't feel the need to perform.

Because of who I happen to be friends with, I've been fortunate enough to experience things that have nothing to do with what I've earned or achieved. I spent my teens brushing shoulders with some of the world's elite—people with money, power, and access most can only dream about. I ended up in rooms I never expected: VIP sections, studio sessions, after-parties.

I was always grateful to be included. It was exciting—but also, oddly isolating in ways I didn't expect. There's something ironic about being surrounded by success... it doesn't make you feel closer to it, it makes you measure yourself against it. And eventually, that feeling of comparison bled into how I saw myself.

People would make comments that fed my insecurities. When they found out who my friends were, they'd say things like, ***"How are you friends with them?"*** or ***"Wow, I can't believe they're friends with you."*** And as innocent as those comments were, they only reminded me that people couldn't understand why I was there. I started to feel like I owed others an explanation. Like I had to justify standing beside my own friends.

I found myself experiencing awkward moments I didn't know how to handle. People would introduce themselves to everyone in the group except me. I was the person the security guard would stop at the door, and my friends would have to turn around and say, ***"No, she's with us."***

I'd meet people multiple times and have full conversations, but the next time I saw them without my famous friends next to me, they'd act like we'd never met. I got used to reintroducing myself. Over and over again.

To be remembered is one of the most fundamental desires of being human. And being forgotten really weighed on me.

Thankfully, as I got older, I grew out of my insecurities and started focusing on things that I was actually good at—like being kind and making people feel seen. I stopped caring about how I was perceived and instead focused on what I could control: how present I was.

Giving someone your genuine undivided attention is a skill. Making someone feel seen is a skill.

Being kind, even when people don't notice or reciprocate, is a skill. Eventually, I was able to master these skills. And when I did, something changed. People started remembering me. Even better, they remembered how I made them feel. They didn't say I was the funniest person they'd ever met or the smartest. They said I was the kindest.

And that meant more to me than anything else ever could.

Kindness might be the most overlooked opportunity we have. It costs literally nothing. It's available to everyone, and its impact is immediate.

A little gesture or the right words at the right time can change the entire direction of someone's day. And the feeling it gives you? *Addictive.* You'll want to do it again. Because in a simple act, you realize you've made someone's life better. And that shit feels really good.

Kindness is my greatest strength. It's the quality I value most in myself. And the thing I get most excited about. I even catch myself thinking about it well before I've said a single word.

Anticipating the moment: like, *this person has no idea that for the next five minutes my only goal is to make them feel seen. To make them smile. To leave them lighter than I found them.*

When I started seeing kindness as an actual practice instead of just a personality trait, it stopped being something I did only when it was convenient and became something I chose even when it was hard.

I would pay attention to the details: a rough day ahead or the project they were excited about in our last conversation. And by doing so, I was able to make people feel seen in ways surface-level interactions never could.

Somewhere along the way I developed a sense of purpose. As if maybe this is my unique contribution to the world. Not talent or status—but making sure people walk away from me feeling better than they did before.

•••

Friendships don't exist in isolation. When you're in a relationship, the people you love will inevitably overlap, and it makes such a difference when your friends and your partner are committed to getting to know one another. It creates a sense of harmony instead of tension, and it allows you to share your life without feeling like you're always juggling two separate worlds.

I've been blessed in that my friends have gone out of their way to not only accept Heydee but to genuinely support and befriend her. They include her in our conversations and invite her to their events. And Heydee has always matched that effort. She's shown up for them. She's encouraged them. And she has ***always*** made space for my friendships to thrive alongside our relationship.

Over time, that mutual effort has led to healthier relationships across my life. Now, Heydee's connections with my friends exist entirely on their own. Ed, for example, has gotten so close to Heydee that they share their own inside jokes and even argue like siblings.

And when Heydee and I have disagreements, he's been able to step in as a mediator: always offering perspective without taking sides. And what makes it especially meaningful is that respect always remains intact. I've vented to Heydee about my friends, and it's never influenced how she treats them. And the same is true in reverse: I've vented to my closest friends about my relationship, and they've never let it change how they perceive or treat Heydee.

I think a common misconception is that people have great friends without putting in the work. But it doesn't work like that. Solid friendships come from a commitment to love each other through the ups and downs, to forgive and move on from mistakes, and to decide the relationship is worth investing in.

It's pretty easy to say you love your friends, but love without time eventually goes unnoticed. The real currency of friendship isn't love—it's presence. Showing up, even in subtle ways, to remind people they matter.

I go out of my way to be a great friend. I ask about their loved ones. I go to their events. I share their work. I celebrate their victories and remind them of their importance after their failures. I push them. I am their biggest fan. I love them through thick and thin. And I tell them that often. Because people deserve to hear it while they're still here to feel it.

I've been more fortunate in friendship than most. Some people pour years into friendships that eventually fall apart, while others wake up one day and realize they were holding on to something that was gone long before they let go.

These moments feel tragic. They hurt. And to make sense of it all, we call it a waste. We tell ourselves it was time misspent or energy misplaced.

Although the explanations we give ourselves may feel comforting in the moment, they can come with a cost. They can make you hesitant to open up again and to invest in new friendships. Even though they feel like protection, these narratives can lead you to build walls where bridges should be.

The biggest disservice we can do to ourselves is letting the pain of past friendships define the ones that haven't begun yet. When you carry old baggage into new relationships, you risk punishing new people for someone else's mistakes. And by doing so, you may be the very thing holding yourself back from a healthy, solid friendship. At some point, you have to decide that new people deserve a clean slate.

So here's your sign to go for it. To reach out. To send the text. To start the conversation. To make friends. And to trust that the right ones will find you at the right time, and stay for the right reasons.

QUESTIONS ***#617 - #661***

Healthy Friendships

Communication & Boundaries

Social Dynamics

HEALTHY FRIENDSHIPS

617.
Do you consider yourself a good friend? What three words do you think your friends would use to describe you?

618.
What do you think are your biggest strengths and your biggest challenges when it comes to being a good friend?

619.
What do you think is the most important quality for maintaining a healthy, long-lasting friendship?

620.
Do you feel like we both show up equally in our friendships? Why or why not?

621.
Do your friends make you feel supported? Who's been there for you the most *(and the least)*?

622.
Do you usually match the energy your friends give, or are you okay with putting more into a friendship even when it's not always reciprocated?

623.
If someone said, *"You're a lot like your friends,"* would you take that as a compliment?

624.
Do all of your friendships bring you joy, or are there some you keep mostly out of comfort or routine?

625.
What's your "love language" when it comes to friendship, and what kinds of gestures mean the most to you in return?

626.
Have you ever watched a friend become a totally different person depending on who they're around—and did that change how you saw them?

627.
Is there a friendship you've outgrown over time? If so, what changed?

628.
Do you believe good friends should check in regularly, or can friendships survive without constant contact?

629.
Do you think it's healthy to be friends with an ex? If so, what kind of boundaries need to be in place for it to work?

630.
What's something a friend has done for you that meant more than they probably realized?

631.
Do you think a "good friend" should always take your side—or challenge you when they think you're wrong?

COMMUNICATION & BOUNDARIES

632.
What types of affection toward a friend would make you uncomfortable, and where do you draw the line?

633.
How would you set boundaries with a friend who shows up uninvited or inserts themselves into plans?

634.
Do you want to know if I've ever had a romantic history with someone who's still in my life? How important is that to you? *(e.g., a friend, coworker, roommate, etc.)*

635.
Are there any topics you think should be off-limits when talking to friends about our relationship?

636.
If I noticed a friend taking advantage of your kindness, would you want me to say something, or stay out of it?

637.
Do I make you feel comfortable enough to ask for one-on-one time with your friends, even if I'm close with them too?

638.
Have you ever lent or borrowed money *(or something important)* to/from a friend? Did it cause any tension or change the dynamic between you?

639.
How would you handle a situation where a friend repeatedly "forgets" to pay you back or always expects you to cover the bill?

640.
How do you feel about keeping certain friend groups separate? Do you think it's okay not to invite everyone to everything?

641.
If a friend repeatedly disrespects your boundaries, how many chances do you give before cutting them off—and how do you decide when it's time to end the friendship?

642.
How do you typically handle conflict with a friend? Do you prefer to talk it out right away or take time to process first?

643.
Are you able to apologize to a friend even if you don't fully feel at fault? Why or why not?

644.
Have you ever found out a friend wasn't honest with you? If so, how did that affect your friendship?

645.
Have you ever had a friendship end because of miscommunication or growing animosity? If so, what do you think could've been done differently?

646.
When was the last time you felt unheard or dismissed by a friend? Did you bring it up or let it go?

SOCIAL DYNAMICS

647.
How should we navigate spending time with friends if you're more introverted and I'm more extroverted?

648.
If you ever felt intimidated by one of my friends *(because they're attractive, flirty, or my type)*, would you feel entitled to ask me not to hang out with them anymore?

649.
Where do we draw the line when it comes to arguing in front of our friends or involving them in our disagreements?

650.
How would you react if your friend came at me sideways, with energy or attitude that felt off or disrespectful?

651.
If your friend consistently depends on you emotionally but never reciprocates, would you continue supporting them?

652.
Do you ever feel left out or excluded in certain friend groups or social dynamics?

653.
Do you ever downplay your success or happiness around certain friends so they don't feel left behind?

654.
If one of our mutual friends was cheating, would you still hang out with them and the person they're cheating on?

655.
What would you do if a mutual friend started flirting with me in front of you? Would you call it out, ignore it, or expect me to handle it?

656.
How much effort do you usually make to connect with the people your friends are dating?

657.
If one of your friends started dating someone you didn't like, would you still feel obligated to support their relationship?

658.
If you became close with someone your friend was dating, and they broke up, would you feel conflicted about staying friends with them?

659.
Do you notice patterns in the types of friends you're drawn to—and what do you think that says about you?

660.
How do you usually handle things when you know you've hurt or let down a friend—and what does taking accountability look like for you in that moment?

661.
Can you call a friend out without fearing the friendship will fall apart—and can you hear hard feedback without taking it personally?

IDENTITY

INTRODUCTION

Most of my childhood, my time was evenly split between two households. I was still in elementary school when my mom and I moved into a room she rented in a seven-bedroom house in the Oakland hills. A few years later, she managed to buy the whole place with a credit card. I'm still not entirely sure how she pulled it off. I just remember people coming to take pictures of it to get it appraised.

The day before, we had gone to Home Depot to buy a tarp so we could cover the roof. We put *"Beware of Dog"* signs everywhere and scattered beer bottles all over the lawn. She told all our neighbors we were hosting an art show… but really, she was trashing the place so it would get appraised at a substantially lower value.

She couldn't afford the house, so we shared a room until I was 16. The other rooms were rented out to all sorts of people: athletes, artists, friends, friends of friends. We always had people crashing on our couch. If someone needed a place to stay, they knew they could come stay with us. Anyone, from childhood homies dealing with problems at home to old men like Wizard who read my mom's tarot cards every week. He lived in People's Park in Berkeley and would stay with us when the weather was bad.

One time, some women from the Olympic cycling team crashed in our living room.

We had guests from all different backgrounds: beliefs, political views, sexual orientations, and ways of living. The environment I grew up in made it normal to coexist with people I didn't always understand or necessarily agree with. It wasn't unusual to walk into the living room and find our roommates in some intense debate. My mom's philosophy was that the more she surrounded me with people who thought differently, the more access I'd have to a wider perspective. And she was right.

From a young age, I witnessed people hold completely different views and still choose connection over division. Over time, I learned that familiarity with difference builds empathy, because it's hard to judge what you've taken the time to understand.

•••

Ashara was my mom's friend. She was an engineer, a pioneer in gender equality, and a trans woman. She taught the world a lot. About technology. About identity. And about what it means to live without apology. She lived on her own terms.

She was also a parent, and I thought her kids were the coolest people ever. Her daughter had a massive sword collection: real samurai swords that looked like they belonged in a museum. I loved spending time with their family. And looking back, I can see how having Ashara in my life at such a young age shaped my empathy.

She wasn't introduced with context or explanation; she was just another adult in my world. A person I looked up to and admired. So when I saw stories about trans people being targeted, it wasn't just something happening *"out there."* It felt close, like it could happen to someone I knew and cared about.

It's harder to ignore injustice once it has a face you recognize.

•••

I was raised by a single mom who was also in school full time for basically half my childhood. Thankfully, she found community: a social club of free spirits and thinkers. Technically, I think it was considered a church. Every Sunday, she'd take me downtown for meditation at 9 a.m., followed by a dance party that went on all morning. And every summer, we all went to Burning Man and camped together.

People wore whatever they wanted. No one cared what anyone else looked like. Everyone just showed up as themselves. I saw all kinds of bodies. Different shapes, sizes, scars, and smiles. And being around that kind of openness from such a young age helped me avoid major insecurities about my own. I had a much more realistic idea of the human body than many of my peers.

I was lucky to be surrounded by a community where everyone was accepted for who they were.

But being raised unconventionally came with contradictions.

Ironically, growing up in such an open environment eventually led me to deny certain truths about myself. I came out late, despite being surrounded by acceptance.

A part of me wanted less attention. My mom was open about her parenting style and we got a lot of shit for it. Especially from other parents. She was the *"crazy"* mom: the weird one who let her kid skip the first week of school every year to go to Burning Man.

She was the last person who'd offer the kind of reassurance other parents were looking for. If someone asked whether she was supervising us, she'd just say *"no. I trust my daughter."*

She rarely gave me rules, only information. She believed that if I understood my choices, I would make the right ones. But that didn't sit well with most parents. And for a while, it didn't sit well with me either. I found myself craving ***"normal"*** more than I craved exploring other sides of myself, like my sexuality.

•••

My unconventional childhood taught me that most things in life exist on a spectrum. Nothing is ever just one thing or another.

Nature itself is proof of this.

Nature runs on gradients. Heat fades, and colors blend. Nothing changes all at once: it all transitions. Everything we know exists somewhere in between.

Across countless species, gender roles are fluid. In some reptiles, sex is determined by temperature. Certain fish switch genders based on their group's needs. Change is evolution. A reminder that identity, like nature itself, is not rigid. It moves. It grows. And at its core, **it's something fundamental.**

Identity is not a choice. It's part of a person's core sense of self. It's not a decision or a preference. It's simply there. For many, transitioning is about bringing that inner truth to the surface. It's alignment. It's about the way someone feels inside, matching how they live and express themselves outwardly.

This is something worth honoring and worth celebrating.

Sadly, not everyone gets the chance to live as their true self. For so many people, the fear of hate crimes, the lack of access to care, or the weight of society's expectations makes authenticity feel out of reach. And today, with increasingly hostile political attacks on our fundamental freedoms, these barriers are only getting stronger.

Across the country, laws are targeting the queer community. From bans on gender-affirming care to the erasure of LGBTQ+ education, our existence is being attacked. We're watching lawmakers turn our identities into talking points, stripping rights from queer people, and spreading fake propaganda about who we are.

Policies are being written to decide which bodies deserve care, what love is acceptable, and which stories are allowed to be told.

These policies restricting access to healthcare, legal recognition, and the right to exist safely have devastating consequences on people's lives.

This is why it's more important than ever, especially within the queer community, to show up for one another. Acceptance alone is not enough. Protection matters. The conversations we have. The advocacy we push for. The space we create for each other: these things dictate the world we live in.

The journey of self-expression and self-discovery is one of the most vulnerable and powerful experiences a person can go through. To be understood in this process, to be met with love instead of resistance, is everything. When we commit to showing up, not just as partners but as friends, as family, and as allies: we do more than offer support. We help build a world where being yourself is no longer a fight, but a birthright.

Identity & Gender Expression

Transition & Support

Partnership Dynamics

IDENTITY & GENDER EXPRESSION

662.
When did you first start exploring your sense of self, and how has it evolved over time?

663.
Who in your life has made you feel the most affirmed and supported? What did that support look like, and what role do they play in your life today?

664.
How did your upbringing or cultural environment influence your sense of identity—whether by offering support or creating challenges?

665.
Are there parts of your identity or expression you haven't felt ready to share with me—and would you feel okay talking about them now?

666.
Are there self-expression rituals, outfits, or styles that make you feel powerful, seen, or more like your true self?

667.
Are there environments or situations where expressing your identity feels unsafe or anxiety-inducing?

668.
What's your favorite way to connect with queer community—dancing, talking, people-watching, flirting, or interacting online?

669.
Do you trust how people interpret your expression, or do you expect them to get it wrong?

670.
When you travel, do you plan how you'll present yourself differently depending on where you're going?

TRANSITION & SUPPORT

671.
What language, names, or pronouns feel most affirming for you?

672.
Are there specific milestones in your transition that you'd like us to celebrate together?

673.
Is there anything you'd like support with *(insurance, DMV, finding affirming doctors)*?

674.
What part of the logistical or practical side of transitioning feels most overwhelming right now—and how can I support you through it?

675.
During this chapter of our life, would a therapist, support group, or outside resource be helpful for one or both of us?

676.
Do you ever feel like I'm holding onto memories or ways of relating that don't fit you anymore? How do you want us to handle photos, memories, or names from the past?

677.
Are there any changes in our connection *(like shifts in attraction, dynamics, or emotional distance)* that you've been thinking about but haven't felt ready to share?

678.
How can I be there for you when you're navigating conversations with people who may not understand your identity yet—whether that's family, friends, or coworkers?

679.
If someone misgenders you or uses the wrong name, would you prefer that I step in or would you rather take the lead?

680.
How do you want to handle sharing your transition journey with extended family or new social circles?

681.
Do you feel comfortable being yourself at work? And do you feel like your workplace policies or benefits support your identity?

682.
Do you ever think about how your identity affects your safety in public, like bathrooms, gyms, or locker rooms? And are there ways I can support you so you feel protected?

683.
Are there countries, states, or cities you avoid because of laws or social climate?

684.
Do we have a system for keeping up with political changes or laws that could put us at risk? And have we talked about what we would do if our rights were threatened where we live?

685.
Are all your legal documents updated to match your name and gender marker? If not, what's still pending?

PARTNERSHIP DYNAMICS

686.
Since starting hormones, how has your relationship with your body changed physically, emotionally, or both?

687.
Has your transition changed how you experience desire or attraction toward me?

688.
How do you feel about physical intimacy now—are there new boundaries or preferences that feel respectful and affirming?

689.
Is there anything I'm currently doing that unintentionally feels unsupportive or unhelpful?

690.
What if your transition changes how others label our relationship—how much do labels matter to us?

691.
What if one of us feels safe expressing our identity in public and the other doesn't—how do we decide whose comfort takes priority in shared spaces?

692.
If your transition means you no longer align with how I identify with my sexuality, how do we navigate this conversation?

693.
How do we balance honoring your process with making space for the changes I may be experiencing as your partner?

694.
What does it look like to move forward as a team, even if we're evolving in separate ways?

PAST RELATIONSHIPS

INTRODUCTION

Whether it's moving in or moving on, movement is a part of life. Leaving a place. Leaving a job. Leaving someone you thought you'd be with forever: it's part of the human experience.

I'm here because my mom left everything she knew and moved across the world. No money or family. No grand plan. Waiting wasn't an option. She had to act. She made a decision and lived with it.

And that decision shaped my whole life.

I'm with Samantha because of all the smaller moves I made before her. The people I dated. The people I hurt. The people who hurt me. Some I cared about and loved. Some I didn't.

I went through fights, flings, and a few breakups that ended on decent terms. But every time I left someone, or someone left me, there was movement. And each of those moves led me to where I am today.

•••

I came out to my mom and friends when I was 13, and had my first girlfriend at 15. Growing up as a lesbian in NYC from 2012 to 2017 was nothing short of wild and unforgettable.

There weren't many lesbian bars—and even if there were, we were way too young to get in.

Instead, you'd find us at house parties in Brooklyn and the Bronx. The walls would sweat, and you knew you had about an hour left when the chairs came out and the lap dances started.

Half the room was hitting the Bronx whine while the other half was locked in on an ex through the thick smoke of hookah.

So many girls, parties, and fights.

The first time I saw Samantha was at one of these parties. She was newly single and just starting to dip her toes into the gay world. She looked a little overwhelmed by it all, but she played it off well.

What she didn't know was that the girl who invited her *(and who she was low-key talking to)* already had a girlfriend. And funny enough, all three of them were there that night.

When I say the gay world can be messy, I mean *messy*. I wanted to go up to her that night, but I didn't. Instead, I found her on Instagram and DM'd her the next day.

Back then, the lesbian world was much smaller than it is today, which also meant you were even more likely to run into your ex. And I did, *more than once.*

There were parties where I'd end up arguing with them, or even their new partner. I was young and let my emotions get the best of me. On the other hand, I had major boundaries crossed with girls I was talking to.

One time, this random girl ***keyed my brand new car*** because I was talking to her ex. I was mad AF. It was a lot.

•••

As I got older, what I wanted started to change.

Eventually the drama died down, and I started dating Samantha. Naturally, I brought some unhealthy patterns with me. For years I excused toxic habits as part of my personality, when in truth they were behaviors I had picked up along the way.

Samantha, on the other hand, moved to New York City when she was eighteen to be with a girl she was dating at the time. Before that, she had a series of situationships. The only other real relationship she had was with someone who was shot and killed during her sophomore year of high school.

That loss rattled her. She developed a fear of losing people she cared about. And because of it, she ended up staying in her next relationship way longer than she should have.

•••

Whether we like it or not, the relationships we've had in our past influence our present and future.

The behaviors we display in our current relationships are often things we learned in our past ones. Regardless of whether you do or don't talk about your past, it shows up. And without context, it's hard to really understand why someone is the way they are.

At the end of the day, it's unrealistic to think you'll never run into your ex.

LGBTQ+ relationships exist in smaller communities. Some exes stay friends and remain in the same social circles. They show up at the same parties. Friend groups and relationships tend to overlap. And boundaries look different for everyone.

What feels normal to you might feel uncomfortable to someone else. Maybe you and your ex are still friends, so checking their Instagram or replying to their mom on your birthday feels fine. Maybe your partner had a bad experience with someone you were involved with. Or they dated someone who dated your ex.

In those cases, even the smallest interactions can cross a line. Or maybe you once tolerated behaviors that wouldn't work for you now. That's why talking about your triggers, your habits, and the things that make you feel wanted *(or unwanted)* is so useful.

Something I've always appreciated about my relationship with Samantha is that she asked about my past early on. She wanted to understand the things I needed in a relationship, as well as the things I didn't like from past ones. We talked openly about what worked, what didn't, and what we each brought to the table. And those conversations saved us from countless arguments later on.

•••

It can be hard to talk about your past.

The last thing anyone wants to do is talk about the fuckups from their last relationship with the person they're with now. But that context can save your relationship.

Maybe they avoid a certain club because that's where their ex used to DJ. Maybe they can't listen to a specific album without feeling sick because it was their breakup soundtrack. Maybe they hesitate to hold hands in public because the last time they did, someone threatened them.

Your partner may pull away when you're upset, not because you did something wrong, but because past experiences made conflict feel unsafe. They might shut down during a fight because silence used to be their only form of protection.

The more context you have, the less everything feels personal. Knowing who your partner was ***before*** helps you appreciate who they are now. And when you understand the story behind a reaction, things just make more sense.

But that understanding has to go both ways. Not sharing your past only makes it harder for them to understand your intentions. You owe your partner the context behind your own behavior. Without that context, they'll fill in the blanks themselves. They'll guess, and they'll usually guess wrong.

Boundaries & Encounters

Memories & Lessons Learned

BOUNDARIES & ENCOUNTERS

695.
Are you still friends with any of your exes? If so, what does that friendship look like now?

696.
Do you think I'm obligated to tell you if an ex reaches out to me? And if we follow each other on social media and they respond to my story, does that count as reaching out?

697.
Do you think it's necessary to unfollow or block exes when you're in a new relationship?

698.
If your ex needed support or was going through something serious, would you feel compelled to be there for them?

699.
Do you think it's appropriate to stay in touch with an ex's family after the relationship ends? Why or why not?

700.
If one of us shares a pet with an ex, what boundaries can we set around that relationship to make sure we both feel comfortable?

701.
Does your life overlap with your ex in any way—through friends, work, or social circles?

702.
Are there certain boundaries we want to set when talking about exes—like details about our sexual dynamics or their personal lives?

703.
Are you comfortable with me bringing up an ex in conversation when it's relevant?

704.
How do you feel about keeping old stuff from exes—like photos, texts, or gifts?

705.
How do you feel about using something intimate *(like toys, lingerie, or music)* that I once shared with someone else?

706.
Are there any exes you'd feel anxious about running into—and if it happens, what's our move: ignore them or say hi?

707.
How do you feel about me hanging out with or being around an ex—especially in group settings *(with or without you present)?*

708.
What would make you feel more uncomfortable—me running into your ex, or you running into mine?

709.
Do you think it's disrespectful for a family member to bring up your ex in front of me?

MEMORIES & LESSONS LEARNED

710.
What was your longest relationship and why did it last, and what was your shortest and why did it end?

711.
Have you ever lived with a partner—what did you learn from it?

712.
Have you ever stayed in a relationship longer than you should have? Why?

713.
What's the biggest red flag you ignored in a past relationship?

714.
Was there a tipping point in a past relationship when it became clear it was over? And is there anything you promised yourself you'd never tolerate again?

715.
Looking back, what do you regret most about how you treated an ex—and what's one valuable thing an ex taught you that you're grateful for?

716.
If you could go back and apologize to one ex, what would it be for?

717.
What habits or flaws did your exes complain about most—and do you think any of those still show up in you now?

718.
What role did your friends or family play in your past breakups?

719.
Have you ever snooped through a partner's phone—what did you find?

BONUS SECTION

INTRODUCTION

Over the years, we have had so many conversations: from early mornings when Samantha reads an article and wants to pick my brain about it, to late-night hypotheticals sparked by some random video we stumbled across online.

Sometimes those chats turn into debates. Sometimes they end in laughs. And other times, they make us pause and really think about why we see the world the way we do.

These are the questions that didn't make it into the main sections: the ones that didn't fit anywhere else, but were too important (or too fun) to leave out.

General Polyamory

Long Distance

Introspective

Random & Fun

Music & Media

Living Together

Would You Rather

GENERAL POLYAMORY

720.
What does polyamory mean to you, and what motivated you to pursue this relationship style?

721.
Do you prefer limited sharing or full transparency about other relationships—and if we do share, what kind of details feel important to you?

722.
What boundaries or agreements do you feel are essential for our relationship?

723.
How do you want to approach sexual health and safety in our relationship and with other partners?

724.
How do you handle feelings of jealousy or insecurity, and how can I support you during such times?

725.
Do you feel comfortable with our current dynamic, or are there any adjustments you'd like to explore?

726.
Do you feel that emotional and practical contributions feel balanced in our relationship?

727.
What's been effective for us in conflict, and what could we improve?

728.
If you could change one thing about our relationship dynamics, what would it be and why?

729.
What does a balanced week or month look like for you in terms of partner time, solo time, and rest?

730.
How do you feel about your partner's meeting or interacting with each other?

731.
Are there any concerns or preferences you have about dating within our shared social circles?

732.
How do you feel about public displays of affection with different partners?

733.
How do we want to approach introducing new partners to our families and friends—and how should we handle it if they're not accepting of our polyamorous relationships?

734.
What are your long-term goals for our relationship, and how does polyamory fit into them?

LONG DISTANCE

735.
Have you done long distance before, and what challenges and unexpected benefits did you notice?

736.
What do you think is a realistic timeframe for being long-distance, and what would make it sustainable?

737.
Are there any temporary circumstances where you would feel comfortable doing long-distance, such as school, military, or a job opportunity?

738.
What are our long-term goals—do we eventually want to live in the same place?

739.
What are your expectations for communication when we're apart?

740.
What feels like the right amount of texting, calling, or facetiming for you—and how flexible is that based on our schedules?

741.
How do you feel about visiting each other or meeting halfway? Would you rather have frequent short visits or fewer, longer trips together?

742.
If one of us moves to another state or city, do you think the person who moved should be responsible for covering the travel expenses for visits?

743.
Are there specific days or times you'd like to set aside for "us time," even if it's just a quick check-in?

744.
How do you feel about maintaining intimacy through virtual means like facetiming or sexting?

745.
How can we celebrate special occasions or milestones while we're apart to make them feel meaningful?

746.
Are there tools or apps *(like shared calendars, love letter apps, games, etc.)* we could try to feel more connected?

747.
What makes you feel jealous or insecure when we're apart?

748.
What signs should we look for that the distance is starting to negatively affect our connection, and how can we course-correct together?

749.
If we had to do long distance tomorrow, what part of our relationship do you think would be tested first—and why?

INTROSPECTIVE

750.
Do you believe everything happens for a reason, or is life random?

751.
What do you think your purpose is—and how did you come to that conclusion?

752.
What do you think happens after we die?

753.
How do you want to be remembered?

754.
When you're debating, how open are you to the possibility that you're wrong? If someone presents new information, how willing are you to change your mind?

755.
When you realize you're wrong, how quickly do you acknowledge it? What does it take for you to reconsider your perspective?

756.
When was the last time you completely changed your mind about something?

757.
Do you think you have a higher IQ or EQ?

758.
When you say someone is "smart," what does that mean to you? What do you view as intelligent?

759.
Do you believe dreams carry meaning or messages—and what's the most bizarre dream you've ever had?

760.
What emotion do you trust the least—and why?

761.
Do you trust your own memories?

762.
If someone you trusted remembered an event differently than you, would you question your memory or theirs?

763.
Do we owe anything to future generations?

764.
If aliens landed here tomorrow and asked you to show them one thing from Earth, what would you pick?

765.
Are there any conspiracy theories you secretly *(or not-so-secretly)* believe in? If so, which ones?

766.
Do you think technology is bringing us closer together or pulling us further apart?

767.
If you could upload your consciousness into a computer, would you?

768.
Do you think AI is ultimately good or bad for humanity?

769.
Is it ethical to build robots that look and act like humans?

770.
Should humans be allowed to edit their children's genes with technology?

771.
Should people be able to turn a person's digital footprint into an AI version of them after death?

772.
Should people have the right to erase their entire digital footprint?

773.
If social media is as addictive as drugs or alcohol, should it be regulated? And should tech companies be legally responsible for the health effects of their platforms?

774.
Should humans have the right to colonize other planets, even if it means displacing potential alien life forms?

775.
If you could know one answer with absolute certainty, what question would you ask?

776.
What do you think will be humanity's biggest challenge over the next 50 years?

RANDOM & FUN

777.
If animals could talk, which species would be the rudest?

778.
If you could have an unlimited supply of one completely random thing (not money), what would it be?

779.
If you could only eat one meal for the rest of your life, what would it be?

780.
If you could swap voices with anyone, whose would you choose?

781.
If you could trade lives with a celebrity for 24 hours, who would it be and what would you do?

782.
What's one thing you've "geeked out" about recently that you wish more people understood or appreciated?

783.
What's a super specific hill you're willing to die on (even if it's totally petty)?

784.
Which voices or noises do you find hardest to tolerate, and why?

785.
What's the one food or flavor that feels deeply nostalgic for you—and can make you unexpectedly emotional the second you taste it?

786.
Are there specific smells that instantly relax you, make you feel sexy, or bring up strong memories?

MUSIC & MEDIA

787.
How important is music in your life, and what impact does it have on you?

788.
How important are TV and movies in your life, and how do they impact you?

789.
Do you ever use music or media as a tool to shift your mood or energy, and if so, what works best for you?

790.
How do you usually discover new music or media, and do you enjoy sharing it with others?

791.
Would you rather never be able to listen to music again or never watch TV/movies again?

792.
What's your favorite song or album of all time? And what's your favorite movie or tv show?

793.
If your life had a theme song or opening scene from a show or movie, what would it be?

794.
What's one song, album, or movie that you think everyone needs to experience at least once?

795.
Are there any shows, movies, or songs you feel shaped your outlook on life?

796.
What's the last piece of media that made you cry?

797.
If you could get tickets to see one artist, who would it be?

LIVING TOGETHER

798.
Do you have any non-negotiable habits or routines at home, like needing the dishes done before bed or making the bed every morning?

799.
What's your preferred noise level at home—music, TV, or quiet? And in the mornings, do you prefer a quiet house or music and conversation?

800.
What's your thermostat comfort zone, and how do we compromise if we're opposites?

801.
How much alone time do you realistically need on a regular basis?

802.
What's your ideal nighttime routine at home?

803.
Are there any quirks or habits you're worried might become irritating once we live together?

804.
Are you comfortable sharing everything *(like clothes, makeup, personal items)*, or do you prefer having "yours" and "mine"?

805.
If I forget to clean something up, would you rather tell me or just do it yourself?

806.
What are your expectations when it comes to keeping shared spaces clean and organized? What's 'clean enough' to you?

807.
If we have different comfort levels around clutter, tidiness, or deep cleaning, are you willing to compromise?

808.
How do you feel about splitting responsibilities for things like meal prep, laundry, or grocery shopping? Would you rather take turns, divide tasks, or decide as we go?

809.
If you ever feel like I'm not pulling my weight with household chores, do you feel comfortable telling me?

810.
How do you want to handle household expenses *(like groceries, cleaning supplies, or furniture)*?

811.
What's your style when it comes to decorating our shared space—minimalism, coziness, or something else? And if one of us wants to change things, how should we make that decision?

812.
If we threw a themed night or holiday event, what's one thing you'd be excited to plan or take over?

813.
How do you feel about having guests over—what feels like too often? And what's the best way to compromise if our moods or energy don't match?

814.
Are you okay with people dropping by unannounced, or do you prefer to know prior?

815.
Are you the type to chat with neighbors and get involved in the community, or do you like to keep things more private at home?

816.
What's one thing your ex did while living together that you absolutely don't want me to repeat?

817.
How do you imagine we'll fight at home—loud and fiery, or cold and quiet? Which scares you more?

WOULD YOU RATHER

818.
Would you rather have to apologize to someone you can't stand or forgive someone who doesn't deserve it?

819.
Would you rather be a big fish in a small pond or a small fish in a big pond?

820.
Would you rather have the ability to teleport anywhere instantly or be able to time travel?

821.
Would you rather have unlimited free concert tickets to see any artist or free access to every movie theater forever?

822.
Would you rather be famous for a talent or skill you have or for an invention you created?

823.
Would you rather be able to talk to animals or speak every human language fluently?

824.
Would you rather always have perfect weather but never experience seasons, or experience all seasons with unpredictable weather?

825.
Would you rather you and your partner have a different taste in music or tv?

826.
Would you rather your group chat messages get leaked or your search history become public?

827.
Would you rather be the subject of a viral meme or accidentally create a cringey viral trend?

828.
Would you rather be friends with your favorite influencer or get free products from their brand for life?

829.
Would you rather meet your favorite celebrity in real life or have them follow you on social media?

830.
Would you rather date someone who's chronically late or someone who's obsessed with being early to everything?

831.
Would you rather cancel your favorite artist for something problematic or defend them even if they're wrong?

832.
Would you rather date someone with a different political view or someone who hates all your favorite media?

833.
Would you rather date someone who overshares details of your relationship online or someone who refuses to acknowledge you on social media?

834.
Would you rather lie to protect a friend who did something wrong or tell the truth and risk ruining their life?

835.
Would you rather take a high-paying job for a company you morally oppose or struggle financially while doing something you believe in?

836.
Would you rather speak up against injustice but lose your friends, or stay silent & preserve your relationships?

837.
Would you rather always know when someone is lying to you, or always be able to get away with a lie yourself?

838.
Would you rather be with someone who constantly needs reassurance—or someone who gives almost none at all?

839.
Would you rather have your partner notice every little thing you do, or never notice anything at all? (nitpicky or oblivious)

840.
Would you rather find out your partner secretly hates your favorite hobby or that they're way better at it than you?

841.
Would you rather be desired but not taken seriously, or respected but rarely desired?

842.
Would you rather vote for a candidate who aligns with your personal beliefs but has no chance of winning, or a less ideal candidate who can realistically beat someone you oppose?

843.
Would you rather be admired for something you didn't earn, or ignored for something you worked your whole life for?

844.
Would you rather always be the smartest person in the room, or the most liked?

845.
Would you rather be seen as intimidating, or be seen as harmless?

846.
Would you rather forget someone's name immediately after meeting them or call them the wrong name confidently?

847.
Would you rather go on a reality show and get portrayed as the villain or be edited out of it entirely like you weren't even there?

Dear Reader,

If you have made it this far, thank you.

Thank you for your time, your presence, and your willingness to show up for the questions that do not always come with easy answers. You have done something meaningful. You took the time to be present and pay attention. To each other, and to yourselves. These conversations are not easy. But the fact that you engaged with them means something. It speaks to your care, your effort, and your courage.

There is no final destination when it comes to understanding each other. People grow and needs change. Love evolves. What matters most is that you continue to lean in with curiosity, with clarity, and with compassion. Your effort is seen. Your presence matters. Keep showing up.

We are rooting for you!

ABOUT THE AUTHORS

Meet Heydee

Heydee was born in Shiraz, Iran, and moved to Queens when she was nine. She speaks Farsi fluently, which I've always admired. Speaking more than one language is so badass.

She works really hard at everything she does. She's been a massage therapist for about eight years, and the job is both physically exhausting and emotionally heavy. People literally hand her their pain. And yet she comes home and still finds the energy to make us dinner.

She is considerate, kind, and compassionate toward people she's never even met, and I love that about her.

When we first met, she had never had a pet. Now, a decade later, she's the most dedicated cat mom I've ever seen. The way she cares for our cats with so much love and attention is just one more reason I fall in love with her over and over again.

We share the same taste in music, which is huge for me. Music is always on in our apartment, and we're always swapping songs and playlists.

We also love watching TV together.

We overlap a lot, but we have our solo stuff too. For example, I save my science documentaries for when I'm alone, and she watches horror movies *(her favorite kind of TV)* when I'm not around.

Cooking is her love language.

She cooks with the kind of love that feels inherited, like it's been passed down through generations of women who knew how to pour themselves into a meal. Her mom is always cooking, and her grandma was too. It definitely feels generational.

She is always open to new ideas: even when I'm rambling about something that makes absolutely no sense. And I love how much she loves to experience life. I'm happy just sitting and talking all day, but she needs activities. She gets me up and doing things.

Her style is fluid: confident in both elegance and comfort. She loves wearing heels and a dress that shows off the body she's worked incredibly hard for—but she also loves my closet. Most of the time, you'll catch her in something I'd wear too.

She loves fitness. One of my earliest memories with her is sitting at the gym with my laptop while she met with her trainer.

I'm so much healthier now than I was when we first started dating, and I have her to thank for that. She's changed our entire lifestyle. She's the reason we work out and take our vitamins. She's always pushed us in a better direction.

She is also really tough. I don't think I've ever seen her scared or even intimidated by anyone. And at the same time, she's also a total crybaby. Watching her lift my body weight at the gym and then tear up over a mildly emotional commercial... that's the duality of Heydee.

I love how seductive she is. That Scorpio tension is no joke.

She's grounded, generous, beautiful, and confident. She smells amazing, always—probably because her perfume collection is one of her most prized possessions. She's always been into scent—from her candle company, Hvāre, to her DIY body oils, to her need to smell literally everything.

She loves me with her whole self. Not just me, but my friends, my family, and the things I care about. Loving her has made my life fuller.

She is, without a doubt, **my glass half full.**

Meet Sammi

When we started writing this book, it felt funny to keep referring to her as "Samantha," since everyone else knows her as Sam or Sammi. But she's always been Samantha to me. Sometimes I'll call her Leila *(her middle name)*, depending on my mood.

Samantha was born and raised in the Bay Area. Growing up, she split her time between her dad's house in Richmond, CA, where she lived with her dad, stepmom, and three siblings, and her mom's place in the Oakland Hills. She moved to New York at 18 and has lived here ever since.

A Leo through and through, Samantha is the person people turn to when they need a pep talk or a reminder of their worth. She always seems to know exactly what to say at the right time. She's also one of the smartest people I know. She's always learning, and usually teaching me something new before I've even had my first sip of coffee in the morning. It's her love language. Chess is another one of her strengths, even if she pretends otherwise.

One of my favorite things about her is how effortlessly she makes me laugh. So much of our time is spent cracking up over the dumbest things. She often has a dad joke ready, and somehow it always lands. Her humor is one of the ways she makes life more enjoyable, and I love that about her.

Samantha is very resourceful.

She's always found unconventional ways to make money while working toward the life she wants. She's a self-taught graphic designer, but has worked just about every kind of job you can think of. No matter what she's doing, she gives it her all.

She takes a lot of pride in being a good person. She shows up for the people she loves and will drop everything to make sure you're okay. She's the first to help a stranger or pick up someone else's trash because she hates when people litter.

We're really different in a lot of ways, especially when it comes to food. I'll eat anything. Samantha has a list of over 130 foods she doesn't like... *with reasons.* But sometimes, if I bug her enough, she'll try something new. Opposites really do attract, and I love that about us. We push each other to experience things we might have never tried on our own.

Then there are the little things that make her ***her***.

She's terrible with directions. She cleans when she's stressed, so the house is always spotless. She's got these big hazel eyes that are so easy to get lost in, freckles that complement them, and a perfect smile.

She still flirts with me like we just met. And she still makes me nervous and gives me goosebumps. She matches my effort. She is my best friend and the love of my life.

She is my favorite person. **My Azizam.**

Made in the USA
Coppell, TX
26 June 2026

83110265R00203